THE SCHOOL OF NUMBERS

WRITTEN BY EMILY HAWKINS
ILLUSTRATED BY DANIEL FROST

WIDE EYED EDITIONS

Welcome to the School of Numbers

STUDENT'S NAME

~~~~~~~~~~~~~~~~~~~~~~~~~~~~

Contents

Term 1

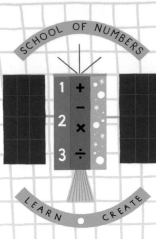

LETTER OF ACCEPTANCE
TO THE

STARSHIP INFINITY
ASTRO ACADEMY

CONGRATULATIONS, CADET

~~~~~~~~~~~~~~~~~~~~~~~~~~~~~~~~

PREPARE TO JOIN US AS
WE EXPLORE THE COSMOS
AND DISCOVER SOME
MATHEMATICAL MARVELS.

The Crew of the Starship Infinity

Welcome Aboard the
Starship Infinity

Greetings, Cadet!

Congratulations on being accepted into our prestigious Astro Academy for math. The *Starship Infinity* is an interstellar research ship roaming the galaxy on a quest for knowledge. Our Astro Academy takes the finest recruits and trains them to be fully fledged crew members. Your lessons will be taught by several leading officers, all experts in their mathematical fields.

We will guide you through three terms, with a total of 40 lessons, on your mathematical journey. In your first term, we will help you get a grip on numbers, in your second term, we will shed light on the secrets of shapes, and in your final term, we will show you how to apply math to the real world around you.

Ready? We can't wait to get started!

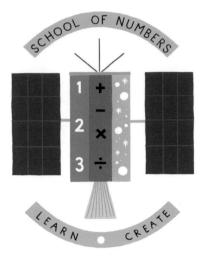

Why Is Math Important?

The world of math is like a playground for your mind. Math allows you to give your brain a workout, making it quicker and sharper. The more you exercise your body, the fitter you get, and it's the same with your brain: the more you use it, the better it works. Math is brilliant for getting those brain cells buzzing.

Math is also important because it helps us solve real-world problems. From reducing traffic jams to designing buildings, from baking cakes to predicting the weather, math is necessary for all sorts of jobs.

For astronauts, math is vital. Without it, we wouldn't be able to build, launch, or navigate our spaceships. You'll find math everywhere in the real world: in nature, in music, and even in art. Because math can be found in so many places, mastering it allows you to understand the world—and it will also help you become amazing at card games and magic tricks!

You can't expect to become an expert overnight though. Mastering math takes practice. You have to start off with the simple stuff before moving on to more complicated areas. Here, aboard the *Starship Infinity*, we will guide you as you embark on your mathematical journey. From basic adding up and taking away to multiplication and division, figuring out fractions and percentages, transforming shapes, understanding probability…we'll be with you every step of the way. If you work hard and practice, you could be captain of your own space cruiser one day!

Before we begin, there are a few important people you need to be introduced to. Turn the page to meet the team!

Meet the Crew

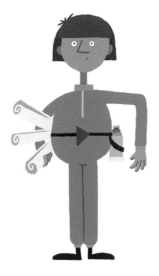

CAPTAIN ARCHIMEDES BROWN

Greetings, cadets. I am your fearless leader, I am your dauntless commander…I am Captain Archimedes Brown. I am an expert in all things mathematical. After all, my love of math is what led me into my career as a space commander. I started out as a humble Astro Academy recruit just like you, cadets, and I worked my way up, climbing the ladder one rung at a time. This is my pet goldfish, Pi. She goes everywhere with me. A word of warning, recruits—I run a very tight ship, and I expect my cadets to arrive on time for all lessons. Jump to it!

LOIS CARMEN DENOMINATOR: FLIGHT OFFICER

It's a pleasure to meet you, cadets. I am the ship's Flight Officer. I am based in the Control Room, where I oversee all aspects of the starship's flight, from launch to piloting, course correction to atmospheric entries. My absolute passion is the study of fractions, and I can't wait to share them with you. What I lack in size, I more than make up for in enthusiasm, and I am seldom seen away from my post. They call me the pocket rocket!

DI AMETER: NAVIGATOR

So nice to meet you. I am the Navigator of the *Starship Infinity*, responsible for plotting our course across the galaxy. I have a love of maps and star charts, and feel it's important to always know where you're heading. I like to be precise in all things—it has been said that I'm a bit of a stickler. My work station is the one where everything is neatly aligned. My piles of paper are straight, and my pens are arranged in height order. In math, my specialization is geometry—I look forward to opening your eyes to the wonderful world of shapes in Term 2, cadets.

AL JABRA:
CHIEF ENGINEER

Hello, my friends! I'm Al, the Chief Engineer. It's my job to make sure the starship is in good working order— that all our systems and equipment are well maintained and ready for action. Although I have a team of engineers working for me, I still like to get my hands dirty. In math, my areas of expertise are algebra and arithmetic. I love problem solving and playing around with numbers, and I'm excited about sparking a love of math in you, too. It's going to be a voyage of discovery!

AVA RIDGE:
DIRECTOR OF RESEARCH

Blistering blackholes, cadets, how wonderful to meet you! My name is Ava, and I am Director of Research. I run the Investigation Station, overseeing all the experiments we conduct on board, along with the research we carry out on foreign planets. I have a love of statistics and am an avid collector of numbers. I adore gathering and cataloging data, from the lengths of different sausages in the Cosmic Cafeteria to the head circumferences of all the crew members. I'm thrilled to welcome you aboard.

ADAM UP:
CHIEF OF SECURITY

Oh, hi. Yep, I'm Adam, Chief of Security. It's my job to ensure the safety of the ship and all its crew members, whether on board or on visits to foreign planets. At the moment, an alien species named Black Hydras are the biggest threat to our security. They rampage around the galaxy making a nuisance of themselves. But I've got them under control! Anyway, I'm going to be teaching you all about arithmetic—adding, subtracting, multiplying. Math is not scary or difficult—we can all be good at math if we believe in ourselves and take it one step at a time.

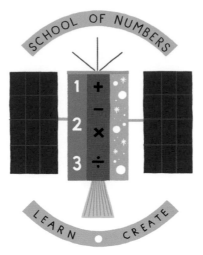

Getting the Knack of Numbers

Welcome to Term 1, new cadets! As part of our first term aboard the *Starship Infinity,* we will be learning all about numbers, and how we can use them in all sorts of useful ways.

Numbers have been around for a LONG time. No one knows exactly when people started using numbers, but 30,000-year-old pieces of bone have been found that have notches on them, which might have been used for counting. Much later—about 5,000 years ago—the clever ancient Egyptians came up with a more advanced system of math, not too different from the system we use today.

Some of the first numbers you heard were probably counted on your fingers and toes…One little piggy, two little piggies…From the moment people started to count, they used their fingers to help them. Did you know that a digit is a number, but it is also a word for a finger? We have ten fingers, so it's no surprise that in our system of math there are ten digits, which make up all the numbers you'll ever need to know. In a moment, you can turn the page to meet these digits.

This term, we'll discover how to use numbers to do all sorts of tricks. You'll stick them together, split them apart, and multiply them until they become bigger and bigger and bigger! Getting a grip on numbers will help you as you climb the ranks of our starship. From comparing quantities of alien spacecraft to figuring out how much rocket fuel you need, or even dividing a pizza in the Cosmic Cafeteria, numbers are everywhere. Master them, and the galaxy will become your mathematical playground. Seat belts buckled? Ready for blastoff? Here we go!

Lesson 1
What are Digits?

My dear cadets, I am delighted to be teaching you your first lesson. Let's begin with the basics—it's as easy as 1, 2, 3.

What are 1, 2, 3? They're numbers, but they're also known as digits. Digits are the building blocks of math.

The thing to remember is that there are only ten of them:

1, 2, 3, 4, 5, 6, 7, 8, 9,

and...what is the tenth digit? Is it 10? Well no, actually, because 10 is made up of two digits: a one and a zero. The tenth digit is zero!

0

WE CAN STICK THESE DIGITS TOGETHER TO MAKE ANY NUMBER: 23, 467, 1,050, 8,495, 5,346...YOU GET THE PICTURE.

Now, listen carefully. The next thing to remember is that the **position** of each digit is important. **Each digit means something different, depending on its position in a number.** Let's put them in boxes to make things easier:

THOUSANDS	HUNDREDS	TENS	UNITS
5	3	4	6

Each of the boxes above is worth ten times as much as the box on its right. The digit farthest to the right tells you how many "units" (or "ones") you have. The next digit to the left tells you how many "tens" you have. The next shows how many "hundreds," the next is the number of "thousands," and so on.

Here, the value of the 5 is five thousands, the value of the 3 is three hundreds, the value of the 4 is four tens, or 40, and the value of the 6 is six ones.

You can always tell a digit's value by its position: the farther to the left it is, the more it is worth.

This system saves us a lot of time. Writing the number 346, for example, is much quicker than making three hundred and forty six little notches on a stick. Thank goodness for digits!

ZIP, ZILCH, ZERO

Let's take a minute to think about nothing. I don't mean take a break and put your feet up! When I say "nothing," I mean the magical number ZERO, or 0. You might think it's worthless, but this neat little symbol is very important. Did you know that in the early days of math, the number zero didn't exist? It wasn't until the 7th century that an Indian mathematician saw the importance of zero. What is the importance of zero, I hear you ask? Let's take a look.

IN THE NUMBER 204, FOR EXAMPLE, THE ZERO TELLS US THAT THERE ARE NO TENS. IF WE DIDN'T HAVE THIS ZERO, THERE WOULD BE NO WAY OF TELLING 204 APART FROM 24, OR OF TELLING THE DIFFERENCE BETWEEN 1,000 AND 1! AND WHAT A CONFUSING WORLD THAT WOULD BE.

ZERO THE HERO

Zero became an international superstar. Its fame spread quickly from India to the Middle East, and then to Europe. But some people were suspicious of the new number. In 1299, the government of the Italian city of Florence actually banned it, because it made accounts easier to fiddle (with a quick stroke of a pen, a zero can easily be made to look like a 6 or a 9). But the force of zero was unstoppable, and by the 1500s it was in common use.

ACTIVITY

Gerald, our onboard zookeeper, is having some trouble making a sign for Edna the Octophant's birthday. She's four thousand and six today! Can you help him pick the right number? Now, where are those candles?

A) 4,060 B) 4,600 C) 4,006

Answer: 4,006. This number has four thousands and six units.

Lesson 2
Making Things Add Up

Hi, cadets, it's me, Adam. Your first lesson is done! It wasn't too hard, was it? Now you've learned about digits, we can start having some fun with them. First, let's look at addition, or adding up, which is my favorite thing to do. Addition means putting numbers together to make a new, bigger number. It doesn't matter what order you add numbers together in. So if there are five Flurglewarpers in a Space Zoomer, and three more get in, there will be eight Flurglewarpers. But if there were three Flurglewarpers in the Space Zoomer, and five more got in, you'd still end up with eight. So 5 + 3 is the same as 3 + 5, and they both add up to 8. We already know that each digit in a number means something different depending on its position, so if you have 574, that means five hundreds, seven tens, and four units. If you want to add 574 to 23, **you need to add units to units, tens to tens, and hundreds to hundreds.**

1. Start by writing the numbers one above the other, making sure the units line up.

IF YOU SEE THIS LITTLE SYMBOL, IT MEANS ADD!

KEEP THOSE UNITS IN LINE, CADETS!

2. Here goes…we need to add up each column, starting with the units. **So, 4 + 3 is 7, so you'd write 7 under the line. Then you move onto the tens: 7 + 2 is 9, so you'd write 9 under the line. And finally, with the hundreds, you don't have anything to add the 5 to, so you just write 5 below the line. Ta-da!**

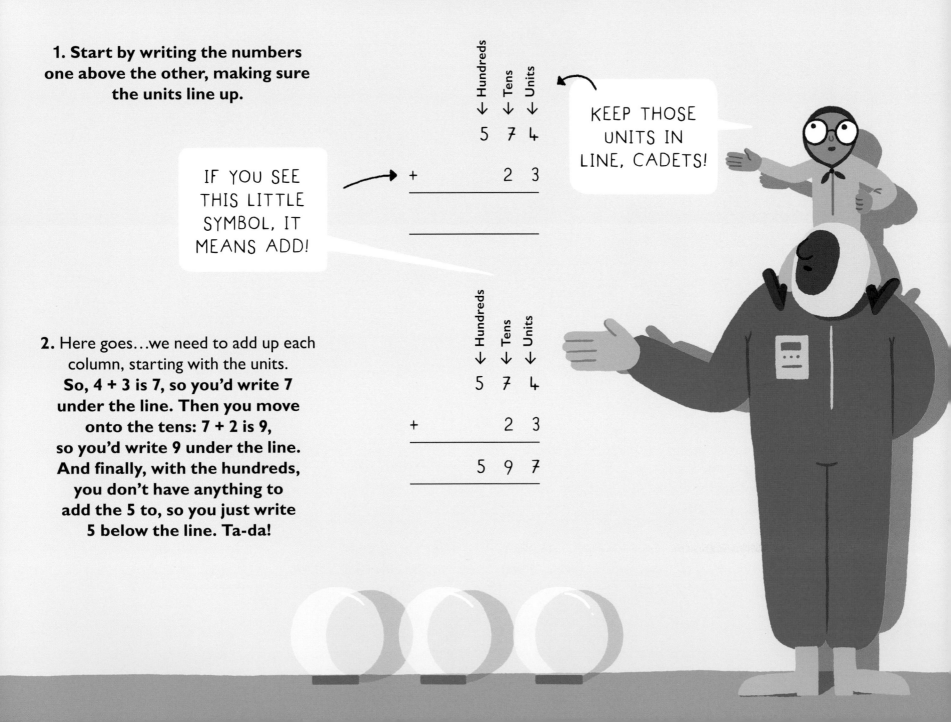

1. The thing to remember here is that if one of the columns adds up to 10 or more, you need to write the right-hand digit of that answer in the column, and carry the left-hand digit to the next column, to the left. Starting with the units column, 7 + 5 = 12, so we put the 2 in the units column, then carry the 1 into the tens column, writing it at the bottom so you don't forget it.

```
    3 6 7
+   1 6 5
_____
        2
_____
        1
```

DONT FORGET ME!

2. Next, when you add up the tens column, remember to include the 1 that you've carried over. So here we have 6 + 6 + 1 = 13. We write the 3 in the tens column and carry over the 1 to the hundreds column.

```
    3 6 7
+   1 6 5
_____
      3 2
      1 1
```

3. Nearly there. Now all we have to do is add up the hundreds column, remembering the carried-over 1. So 3 + 1 + 1 = 5. Write that 5 in the hundreds column to give you your answer: 532. Phew, well done.

```
    3 6 7
+   1 6 5
_____
    5 3 2
      1 1
```

MENTAL MATH TIP

Sometimes, you need to add things up quickly, so it's good to practice adding up in your head. You might find it easier to add whole groups of ten, rather than complicated numbers with itty bitty units. So if you have to add up 33 + 46, put the units to one side for a moment and just do 30 + 40, which gives you 70. Then add the 3 and 6 at the end, giving you 79. Easy!

ACTIVITY

Mumbo and Squurgle are on their way to the Alien Outfitters store to buy some gloves. Mumbo has 16 arms and Squurgle has 38. How many gloves will they need to buy altogether?

Take-Away-Tastic

Righty-ho, cadets, for your next lesson, we're going to learn about taking away, or subtraction, which is the exact opposite of addition. "Hang on," I hear you cry, "why do I need to learn subtraction to be a space commander?" Well, if you have a fleet of 76 spacecraft, and 58 get swallowed by a black hole, a smart commander needs to know how many will be left.

1. To take 58 away from 76, write the two numbers down, with the larger number on top. **Remember to keep those units lined up, just as we did with adding.** The same rule applies here: you take units away from units, tens away from tens—you get the gist.

2. Start with the units column. How do you take away 8 from 6? That seems impossible, because 8 is bigger than 6. What you need to do is borrow 10 from the tens column. So the 7 in the tens column changes to a 6, and the 6 in the units column becomes 16...

3. That's better. Now we can take 8 away from 16, giving us 8. And in the tens column, we take 5 away from 6, which leaves us with a 1 to write underneath.

$$
\begin{array}{r}
{}^{6}\!\not{7}\ {}^{1}6 \\
-\quad 5\ \ 8 \\
\hline
 \\
\end{array}
$$

$$
\begin{array}{r}
{}^{6}\!\not{7}\ {}^{1}6 \\
-\quad 5\ \ 8 \\
\hline
1\ \ 8 \\
\end{array}
$$

THIS LITTLE SYMBOL IS A MINUS SIGN. WHEN YOU SEE IT, GET READY FOR SOME SUBTRACTION ACTION.

THERE WE GO: 18 SPACECRAFT ARE LEFT.

MENTAL MATH TIP

Here's a handy trick to help you subtract numbers in your head: if you don't like subtracting one number from another, you can figure out what you need to add to the smaller number to get the bigger number. This time, to figure out how many spacecraft are left, we just need to count up from 58 until we get to 76. Something like this: 58 + 2 = 60, 60 + 10 = 70, 70 + 6 = 76. Altogether, we've added on 2 + 10 + 6, which equals 18. So 18 spacecraft escape the black hole!

ACTIVITY

Try out this spooky subtracting puzzle...
1. Choose a four-digit number (it must have at least two different digits).
2. Arrange the digits in order from highest to lowest, then lowest to highest.
3. Subtract the smaller number from the bigger one.
4. Repeat steps 2 and 3 with your new four-digit number. Then repeat again. Eventually you'll end up with the number 6,174, and, if you repeat the steps, you'll keep getting 6,174 over and over again. The spooky thing is, this works for every four-digit number. Amazing, isn't it?

Lesson 4
What Are Negative Numbers?

How positive are you feeling about negative numbers, cadets? Don't worry! Today we're paying a visit to our Biodome to learn all about them. **Negative numbers are numbers that are less than zero.** They're easy to spot because they've always got a minus sign in front of them. Take a look at the number line. Above the water, all the numbers are positive, and below the water, the numbers are negative. The higher we climb, the higher the numbers go, and the deeper we dive, the lower the numbers get. You'll see that -3 is a higher number than -9, because it's further up on the number line. You can use the number line to help you figure out sums. If a Jabberbird is flying along at 10 feet above the surface, and it dives 16 feet down to catch a tasty Squimmer, what depth will it be at now? All you have to do is count 16 spaces down from 10… so you'll end up at -6 feet.

10 —
9 —
8 —
7 —
6 —
5 —
4 —
3 —
2 —
1 —
0 —
-1 —
-2 —
-3 —
-4 —
-5 —
-6 —
-7 —
-8 —
-9 —
-10 —

MENTAL MATH TIP

A useful fact to remember is that **taking away a negative number is the same as adding.** So, if you see two minus signs next to each other, you can switch them for a plus sign. 8 - (-6) looks a bit frightening, but actually, it means exactly the same as 8 + 6. Phew!

ACTIVITY

A Flying Finfish is swimming along at a depth of -4 feet. It leaps up 6 feet, then dives down 12 feet. What depth is the Finfish at now?

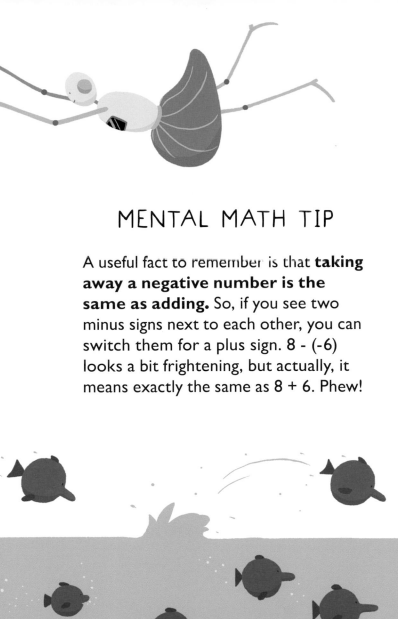

Answer: -10 feet.

Lesson 5
Feel the Freeze!

Brrrr, it's a bit nippy in here! Welcome to the Biodome's Polar Zone, where we'll find out a bit more about negative numbers. You probably already know that a thermometer is a way of measuring temperature: how hot or cold something is. In the 1700s, a clever Swedish astronomer named Anders Celsius came up with a temperature scale that we still use today. On the Celsius scale, zero degrees (0°) is the freezing point of water. Anything colder than this is a negative temperature. Celsius is used throughout much of the world, though another system, Fahrenheit, is used in some places, including the U.S

STRANGE BUT TRUE...

On Celsius's original scale, he set 0° as the boiling point of water and 100° as the freezing point: the reverse of the scale is what we use today!

120°C (250°F) SUNNY SIDE OF EARTH'S MOON
When it gets hot on the moon, it gets *really* hot. But compare this to the core of the sun, which is so hot it's off the scale, at around 15 million°C (27 million°F)!

100°C (212°F) BOILING POINT OF WATER

70°C (158°F) HOTTEST PLACE ON EARTH
Satellites measured this whopping temperature in the Lut Desert in Iran. Scorching!

0°C (32°F) FREEZING POINT OF WATER
Water turns to ice at 0°C. Anything lower than this is called "below freezing."

-93°C (-135°F) COLDEST PLACE ON EARTH
On the East Antarctic Plateau, temperatures can get pretty chilly!

-170°C (-274°F) DARK SIDE OF EARTH'S MOON
Temperatures plummet on the shady side of the moon. Astronauts have to wear protective suits to stop them getting too cold.

ABSOLUTE ZERO
This is the coldest temperature possible in the entire universe! Nothing on Earth has ever gotten this cold.

-273°C (-460°F)

ACTIVITY

You are helping out at the Interstellar Vacations travel agency on the planet of Novaterra, where the usual temperature is 40°C (104°F). A family of Icebiters wants to visit a planet where the temperature is about -120°C (-184°F). Look at this list of planets to help them find the perfect destination.

- Minotropia: 20 degrees hotter than Novaterra
- Squark: 140 degrees colder than Novaterra
- Glaculia: 160 degrees colder than Novaterra
- Ignopolis: 180 degrees hotter than Novaterra
- Sector III: 120 degrees colder than Novaterra
- Olympia: 20 degrees colder than Novaterra

Answer: The planet of Glaculia is the ideal holiday spot for the Icebiters, with an average temperature of -120°C (-184°F).

Lesson 6
Learn to Master Multiplication

Let's talk multiplication. Think of it as the same as adding up. Imagine you're at an Intergalactic Summit and, at lunchtime, seven of the ambassadors eat four sandwiches each. That's seven fours, or 4 + 4 + 4 + 4 + 4 + 4 + 4, which equals 28. Adding up all these fours takes ages, so it's easier to say seven times four (7 × 4) is 28. **It doesn't matter which way you multiply things—you'll always end up with the same answer.** So if four ambassadors eat seven sandwiches each (4 × 7), we end up with the same total: 28. There's no way around it—you must know your times tables! The table will help, and there are a few tips to help remember the hard ones.

Use this table to multiply any two numbers between **1** and **10**. To figure out what 3 x 4 is, look along the 3 row and down the 4 column to find the answer: **12**.

If you struggle to remember that 7 × 8 = 56, then think of it like this: 56 = 7 × 8, or five, six, seven, eight!

All the numbers in the five times table end in 5 or 0.

	1	2	3	4	5	6	7	8	9	10
1	1	2	3	4	5	6	7	8	9	10
2	2	4	6	8	10	12	14	16	18	20
3	3	6	9	12	15	18	21	24	27	30
4	4	8	12	16	20	24	28	32	36	40
5	5	10	15	20	25	30	35	40	45	50
6	6	12	18	24	30	36	42	48	54	60
7	7	14	21	28	35	42	49	56	63	70
8	8	16	24	32	40	48	56	64	72	80
9	9	18	27	36	45	54	63	72	81	90
10	10	20	30	40	50	60	70	80	90	100

Here's a pattern to help you remember the even numbers up to ten in the six times table…
2 x 6 = 1**2**
4 x 6 = 2**4**
6 x 6 = 3**6**
8 x 6 = 4**8**

He ate (8) and he ate (8) till he stuck in the door… 8 times 8 is 64!

ACTIVITY

The order in which you multiply numbers doesn't matter, so 1 x 2 x 3 x 4 is the same as 4 x 3 x 2 x 1! Try it for yourself on a calculator.

You have four fleets of 325 spacecraft. What total number of spacecraft do you command?

1. Put the bigger number on top and start by multiplying the units: 5 × 4 = 20. Put 0 in the units column and carry 2 to the tens column, writing it underneath.

2. Move on to the tens column: multiply the 2 by 4, to get 8. Then add any carried-over numbers to your answer. Here you'd add 2 to your 8. That makes 10, so put the 0 in the tens column and carry the 1 to the hundreds column.

3. Finally, figure out the hundreds: 3 × 4 gives you 12. Then remember to add the carried-over 1, leaving you with 13. The 3 goes in the hundreds column and the 1 is carried to the thousands column. So the answer is 1,300. Give yourself a gold star!

```
  H  T  U
  3  2  5
X        4
---------
        0
     2
```

```
  H  T  U
  3  2  5
X        4
---------
     0  0
  1  2
```

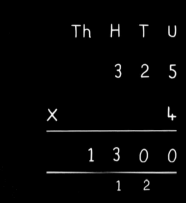

```
Th  H  T  U
    3  2  5
X          4
-----------
 1  3  0  0
    1  2
```

LONG MULTIPLICATION

When multiplying two numbers together that both have two or more digits, things get a bit more complicated. If you were put in charge of 23 fleets of 325 spacecraft, how many spacecraft would you control? Just figure out 325 x 3 and 325 x 20, then add them together.

1. First of all, figure out 325 × 3:

2. Now do 325 × 20. We're dealing with tens now (20 is two tens) so put a zero in the units column. Figure out 5 × 2, which gives you 10. Write the zero in the tens column and carry the 1 to the hundreds column. Next, do 2 × 2, which is 4, adding the carried-over 1 and writing 5 in the hundreds column. That leaves you with 3 × 2, giving you 6 for the thousands column.

3. Then just add your two answers together, giving you a grand total of 7,475 spacecraft. Hurrah!

```
  H  T  U
  3  2  5
X        3
---------
  9  7  5
     1
```

```
Th  H  T  U
    3  2  5
X       2  0
-----------
 6  5  0  0
    1
```

```
Th  H  T  U
    3  2  5
X       2  3
-----------
    9  7  5
 6  5  0  0
-----------
 7  4  7  5
    1
```

Lesson 7
Sneaky Shortcuts

Now, cadets, it's over to me, Ada, to teach you some handy hints. Does multiplying make your brain feel as if it's been whirled around a black hole? Tricky calculations can make my rivets freeze right up…so it's lucky I have these clever shortcuts up my sleeve!

FINGER MULTIPLICATION

You can use your fingers to count on, but did you know that you can also use them for multiplying? Once you remember the simple rules, you'll easily be able to remember your times tables from six to nine.

First of all, imagine that the fingers on each hand are numbered—the little fingers are 6, going up to 10 for the thumbs at the top.

To find out what 7 × 8 is, for example, simply touch the 7 finger from one hand to the 8 finger on the other. Then count the number of fingers below the touching fingers (and the touching fingers too).

There are 3 fingers below the touching fingers, plus 2 fingers touching, which gives you 5. Multiply this number by 10, which gives you 50. Next, multiply the number of fingers above the touching finger on the left hand by the number of fingers above the touching finger on the right.

Here that would give us 3 × 2, which is 6. Now, just add the two parts of your answer together: 50 + 6 = 56, so 56 is your answer!

LIGHT SPEED NINE TIMES TABLE FINGER TRICK

This is a simple way of remembering the nine times table. Imagine your fingers were numbered from 1 to 10. If you wanted to figure out 4 × 9, you'd simply count how many fingers are on the left of the fourth finger: in this case, it's 3. Then count the number of fingers on the right of the fourth finger: here, it's 6. Then just put these two digits together to give the answer: 36!

And did you know that when you add together the digits of any number in the nine times table, you always get nine? So 2 × 9 = 18. And 1 + 8 = 9. Similarly 3 × 9 = 27. And 2 + 7 = 9. Pretty nifty, huh?

MULTIPLYING BY ELEVEN

The 11 times table is a breeze! Two times 11 is 22, three times 11 is 33, four times 11 is 44…easy! But what happens when we multiply 11 by a number bigger than 10? What's 43 times 11, for example?

Just add together the two digits of the number (4 + 3 = 7), then put that number in the middle of the other two (473). But watch out if the two digits add up to 10 or more. With 67 × 11, we'd add 6 and 7 to give us 13. Then you need to put the 3 in the middle and add the 1 to the first number, so the answer would be 737.

STRANGE BUT TRUE

111,111,111 × 111,111,111 = 12,345,678,987,654,321

The answer reads the same forward and backward! You can also try this out for smaller numbers. For example, 1111 × 1111 = 1234321.

3   2   3   5   6   7   8   9   6
    1   4   10

ACTIVITY

Splodge can clean 6 panes of glass on the Observation Deck in 1 minute. In 7 minutes, how many panes of glass can Splodge clean? Use finger multiplication to help you figure this out.

Answer: Splodge can clean 42 windows in 7 minutes, because 6 × 7 = 42.

Lesson 8
Dealing with Division

In this lesson, it falls to me, your valiant captain, to lead you into the sometimes-daunting world of division. Together, we will fend off these feisty sums just as easily as a highly trained space ranger would zap a Black Hydra.

So what is division? **Just think of it as sharing.** Let's say that I have 20 medals to share equally between five worthy officers. The number of medals that each officer gets is 20 divided by five, or 20 ÷ 5, which is 4. I could write it out like this:

LOVELY LEFTOVERS

Imagine that instead of 20 medals, I had 23. Each cadet would still get four medals, but there would be three left over. We call the leftover part the "remainder." And we'd say 23 ÷ 5 = 4 with remainder of 3.

DIVIDING IN YOUR HEAD

The trick here is to remember that **dividing is the opposite of multiplying.** Remembering your times tables will help you here. With 20 ÷ 5, you need to remember that 20 is the same as 5 × 4, so there are four fives in 20…so 20 divided by 5 is 4. Or with 63 ÷ 9, remember that 9 × 7 = 63, so the answer is 7.

WRITING IT DOWN

Sometimes you'll need to write down a sum to get a grip on it. Imagine the students of the Astro Academy were taking a field trip to the planet Novaterra. There are 540 students, and each shuttle can carry 12 students. How many shuttles will we need to carry all 540 students? This is a division sum in disguise! To figure out the answer, you will need to divide 540 by 12.

REMEMBER THESE RULES:

- Start on the left
- Divide into the big number one column at a time
- If the number on the left won't divide exactly into the number on the right, carry the remainder to the next column on the right
- If the number on the left won't divide into the number on the right at all, put a zero on top and carry the whole digit across to the next column along

ACTIVITY

You are cleaning up the equipment room. You have 275 space suits to hang neatly on 11 rails. Each rail must have the same number of space suits on it. How many space suits should you put on each rail?

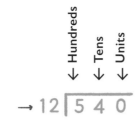

1. With adding, subtracting, and multiplying, you always begin with the units first, **but with division we start at the other end!** In this sum, we start with the hundreds column, so we need to figure out how many times 12 goes into 5.

2. It doesn't take long to realize that 12 doesn't go into 5—it's too big. So we put a zero on the top and carry the 5 one place to the right.

3. Next, we move on to the tens column, where we need to figure out how many times 12 goes into 54. If you know your 12 times tables, you'll remember that $12 \times 4 = 48$. So 12 goes into 54 four times, with a remainder of 6. Write 4 on top, and carry the 6 to the next column.

4. Moving on to the units column, we have to figure out how many times 12 goes into 60. From the 12 times tables, we know that $12 \times 5 = 60$, so the answer is 5. Write that on top, and you have your answer. We will need 45 shuttles to transport 540 cadets to Novaterra.

Answer: You should put 25 suits on each rail.

Lesson 9
How Can We Make Division Easier?

So, the captain has been trying you out on division, has he? How are you getting on? Don't worry—there are a few simple ways to make dividing easier. Learn these tricks, and you'll soon be able to do lots of dividing sums in your head.

$$80 \div 16$$

$$40 \div 8$$

DIVIDING BY 10, 100, OR 1,000

To divide a number by 10, just move the digits one place to the right. For example, to divide 70 by 10, you shift the 7 from the tens column into the units column, giving you an answer of 7. Here are some more:

$90 \div 10 = 9$, $460 \div 10 = 46$, $2,000 \div 10 = 200$

When you divide by 100, you shift the digits two places to the right, and to divide by 1,000 you shift everything three places to the right. So...

$300 \div 100 = 3$, $18,000 \div 1,000 = 18$

Simple!

ZAPPING DIVIDING SUMS

You can think of division as sharing, but you can also think about it as zapping numbers to make them shrink. **If the numbers on both sides of the dividing sum are even numbers, you can zap them to divide them by two.**

With the sum 80 ÷ 16, you can divide both numbers by two (which is the same as halving them), to turn the sum into 40 ÷ 8, which looks much more manageable. Since both sides are still even, why not zap them again? 40 ÷ 8 becomes 20 ÷ 4, which becomes 10 ÷ 2, which is 5. And there's your answer: 80 ÷ 16 equals 5!

Just remember to do the SAME THING (dividing by two) to BOTH SIDES of the sum, and you'll be fine.

ACTIVITY

Can you use your ray gun to zap the sum 96 ÷ 24? Keep dividing both sides by two until the sum is simple enough for you to figure out the answer.

Answer: When you zap both sides by two, 96 ÷ 24 becomes 48 ÷ 12, which shrinks down to 24 ÷ 6, which shrinks to 12 ÷ 3, which is 4.

DIVIDING BY THREE

There's a super-easy way to check if a number can be divided by three. **If the digits add up to a number that can be divided by three, then the number itself can be divided by three.** So with the number 156, add 1 + 5 + 6 to give you 12. You know 12 is in your three times table, so 156 can be divided by three. Neat, isn't it?

20 ÷ 4

10 ÷ 2

MORE ZAPPING

Sometimes, you might want to zap just one side of a sum. Take the sum 156 ÷ 3; it might not seem easy to work this out in your head, but the trick is to split the number 156 into smaller chunks that can easily be divided by 3. In your head, you might be able to figure out that 156 is the same as 150 + 6. Both of these numbers are easy to divide by three: 150 ÷ 3 = 50 and 6 ÷ 3 = 2. So 156 ÷ 3 = 50 + 2 = 52.

ACTIVITY

By adding up the digits of each number, can you tell which of these numbers are divisible by three?
747
2005
942
68

Answer: 747 and 942 are both divisible by three.

Lesson 10
Number Tricks

There you are, cadets! I'm on my way down to the engine room. On the way, I'll tell you about an amazingly talented German mathematician, Carl Friedrich Gauss—he was probably one of the greatest mathematicians of all time. At school, the story goes that Carl would annoy his math teacher by correcting him. One day, the teacher asked the class to add up all the numbers from one to a hundred, thinking it would take them ages. But the teacher was flabbergasted when, only a few moments later, the eight-year-old Carl shouted out the answer—5,050!

So how did he do it? Instead of adding $1 + 2 + 3 + 4 + 5 + 6$, all the way up to 100, you can add the numbers in pairs. If you add the first and the last numbers, the second and the second to last, and so on, you'll notice that: $1 + 100 = 101$, $2 + 99 = 101$, $3 + 98 = 101$... Each of these number pairs adds up to 101. And how many of these pairs are there? You'll realize there are 50. So all you need to do now is multiply 50 by 101, giving you your answer: 5,050. Clever Carl!

The neat part is, this doesn't only work for numbers up to 100, but you can use it to add up all the numbers from one to any number! **You just have to add up the first and the last number, then times this total by half of the last number.**

ACTIVITY

Using Carl's trick, can you quickly add up the numbers from 1 to 10? Now try adding the numbers from 1 to 50.

Answer:
The numbers from 1 to 10 add up to 55. If you add up the first and last number, this is $1 + 10 = 11$. Now figure out half of 10, which is 5. Next, multiply 5 by 11, giving you 55.

The numbers from 1 to 50 add up to 1275:
$1 + 50 = 51$
$50 \div 2 = 25$
$51 \times 25 = 1275$

$1 + 2 + 3 + 4 + 5 + 6 + 7 + 8$
$= 5050$

Think of a number—your coins are in the bag!

PREDICTION TRICK

Ask someone to think of a two-digit number and to secretly write it down. Next, ask them to tell you what the two digits add up to. Imagine they wrote 59; the digits would add up to 14. In your head, multiply that number by 11 (using the shortcut we learned in Lesson 7). Then write down this answer as your secret prediction: in this case, it would be 154.

Ask your friend to reverse their secret number, writing the new number under the first number. Then they need to add the two numbers together. So if they started with 59, they would reverse this to get 95. Then they'd add 59 to 95, which makes 154. It's time to reveal your prediction, and bask in glory!

THINK OF A NUMBER

Here's another prediction trick. See if you can figure out how it works.

Think of a number. Double it. Now add eight. Then divide by two. Finally, take away the number you first thought of. Your answer is 4!

HOW DOES IT WORK?

This is a wonderfully simple trick. To help you understand it, let's imagine that we're thinking about cosmic coins, and I have given you a bag to put yours in, so I can't see them.

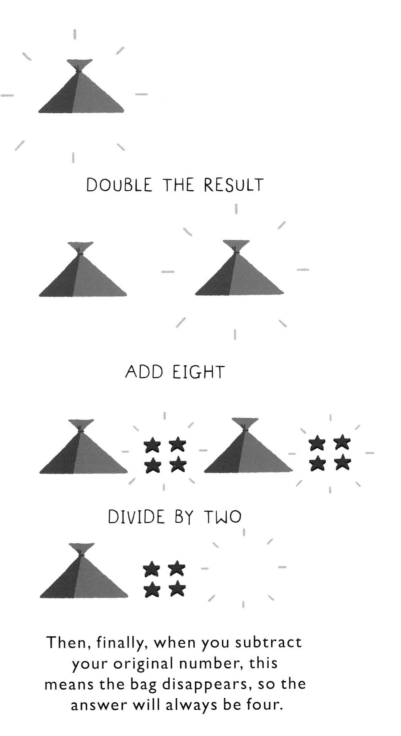

DOUBLE THE RESULT

ADD EIGHT

DIVIDE BY TWO

Then, finally, when you subtract your original number, this means the bag disappears, so the answer will always be four.

EASY!

Lesson 11

What Is a Prime Number?

Listen carefully, cadets—we're very excited to be teaching you about a very special group of numbers: the prime numbers. These mysterious numbers have been puzzling and befuddling mathematicians for thousands of years. So, what is a prime number? **A prime number is a number that can only be divided by one or itself.**

Here are the first few prime numbers: 2, 3, 5, 7, 11, 13, 17, 19, 23, 29…the list goes on. In fact, over 2,000 years ago in ancient Greece, a mathematician named Euclid managed to prove that **the list goes on forever.** There are an infinite number of primes. The strange thing about prime numbers is that they don't appear to follow any obvious pattern—they are scattered

randomly along the number line. It's hard to tell whether a large number is a prime or not without a computer to divide it for you. Hundreds of years ago, mathematicians argued about whether the number 1 was a prime number. These days, most of them agree 1 is not a prime number! Here are some more useful rules…

1

2

3

4

- The only even prime number is 2 (all other even numbers can be divided by 2, so they are not primes).

- All prime numbers except 2 and 5 end in 1, 3, 7, or 9, but not ALL the numbers ending in 1, 3, 7, and 9 are primes (for example, 33 is not a prime number, because it can be divided by 3 and 11).

- If you take any even number bigger than 2, you can always find two prime numbers that add up to it. Let's look at the number 12. We can get 12 by adding together 7 and 5, which are both primes.

- If you take any number bigger than 1 and times it by 2, there will always be a prime number between the first and second numbers. Try it for yourself.

- The largest prime number discovered so far has over 22 MILLION digits! There are many more waiting to be discovered.

- Any number bigger than 1 is either a prime number OR it can be built by multiplying primes together. Take a look at this…

← Prime   ← Prime   ← Prime

2   3   4 (2 × 2)   5

6 (2 × 3)   7   8 (2 × 2 × 2)   9 (3 × 3)

Prime →

In this way, prime numbers are building blocks for the rest of math. That's why we mathematicians love them so much!

5

6

7

8

ACTIVITY

Follow the prime numbers to help the Space Zoomer navigate the asteroid field and find its way back to the Starship.

Answer: Follow the path indicated by the prime numbers 2, 3, 5, and 7.

Lesson 12
Square Numbers and Square Roots

Now you've learned all about prime numbers, it's time for another kind of number: a kind that I find much neater than messy primes…square numbers. **A square number is what you end up with when you multiply a number by itself.** Two times two is four, so four is a square number. Three times three is nine, so nine is a square number.

They're called squares because if you laid them out in rows, they would make exact square shapes. If we look at the windows on the greenhouses in the Biodome, you'll see what I mean…

If you see a number, let's say a 5, with a tiny 2 hovering above it, that's a short way of writing five squared. So 5^2 is the same as 5×5, which is 25.

SQUARING TRICK

I'm going to show you a sneaky trick that will allow you to square any two-digit number ending in a 5 in your head. Imagine you wanted to know the square of 15. You start with the first digit and multiply it by the next highest number. So here, we multiply one by two: $1 \times 2 = 2$. Then all you need to do is stick 25 on the end, giving you 225. Easy!

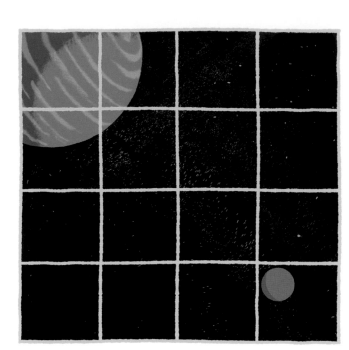

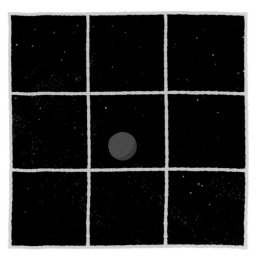

$4 \times 4 = 16$

$3 \times 3 = 9$

$2 \times 2 = 4$

ACTIVITY

Using the Squaring Trick technique, can you figure out the square of 35 in your head? Then check your answer on a calculator.

Answer: The square of 35 is 1,225. This is how you figure it out: $3 \times 4 = 12$, then stick 25 on the end, giving you 1,225.

Let's look at the veggies growing in the Biodome. Above the ground, you can see a neat row of square numbers. Below the ground, you'll notice that each of these numbers has a root. **The square root of a number is the number that, when multiplied by itself, makes the square number.**

REAL-WORLD SQUARE ROOTS

Just say it—why would I ever need to figure out a square root? They crop up quite a lot! Imagine you've landed on a new planet. You've been told to mark out the foundations of a research base that needs to cover 3,600 square feet (see p.67). It's quite difficult to imagine how big that is, isn't it? If you understand square roots, you can figure out that the square root of 3,600 is 60 (because 60 × 60 = 3,600). So, if you wanted a square research base, each side would have to measure 60 feet.

Finding the square root of a number can be tricky, so this is when a calculator comes in useful. On a calculator, you might see a symbol that looks like this ($\sqrt{}$)—that's the square root button. Punch that button, punch in a number and the equals button, and you'll get your answer. But there's a trick for figuring this out without a calculator. All you do is subtract the odd numbers (1, 3, 5, 7, and so on) in order until you get to zero, then count up the number of steps it took to get there. So to find the square root of 49, here's what we'd do:

$49 - 1 = 48$
$48 - 3 = 45$
$45 - 5 = 40$
$40 - 7 = 33$
$33 - 9 = 24$
$24 - 11 = 13$
$13 - 13 = 0$

That took us seven steps, so you know that the square root of 49 is seven.

4

9

16

25

2

3

4

5

Lesson 13
What Are Triangular Numbers?

Welcome to the Investigation Station! **I'm going to teach you about triangular numbers—numbers that make triangle shapes.** Some creatures called Furballs are going to help in this lesson. There's a pattern to these numbers...The first triangular number is made up of one Furball—it's so small it doesn't even look like a triangle. The second triangle has two more Furballs, so it's $1 + 2 = 3$. For the third triangle, we've added a row of three: $3 + 3 = 6$.

The fourth triangle has another row with four more: $6 + 4 = 10$...and so on. For the fifth triangle, we add another five, making 15, and for the sixth triangular number we'd add 6, giving us 21. See the pattern?

There's a simple way of figuring out triangular numbers—it's the same trick we used to add up all the numbers from 1 to 100 in Lesson 10. The fourth triangular number is half of 4 multiplied by 5, the fifth triangular number is half of 5 times 6, the sixth triangular number is half of 6 times 7, and so on. So, what would the 20th triangular number be? Just use the same technique: half of 20 multiplied by 21, or 10×21, which equals 210.

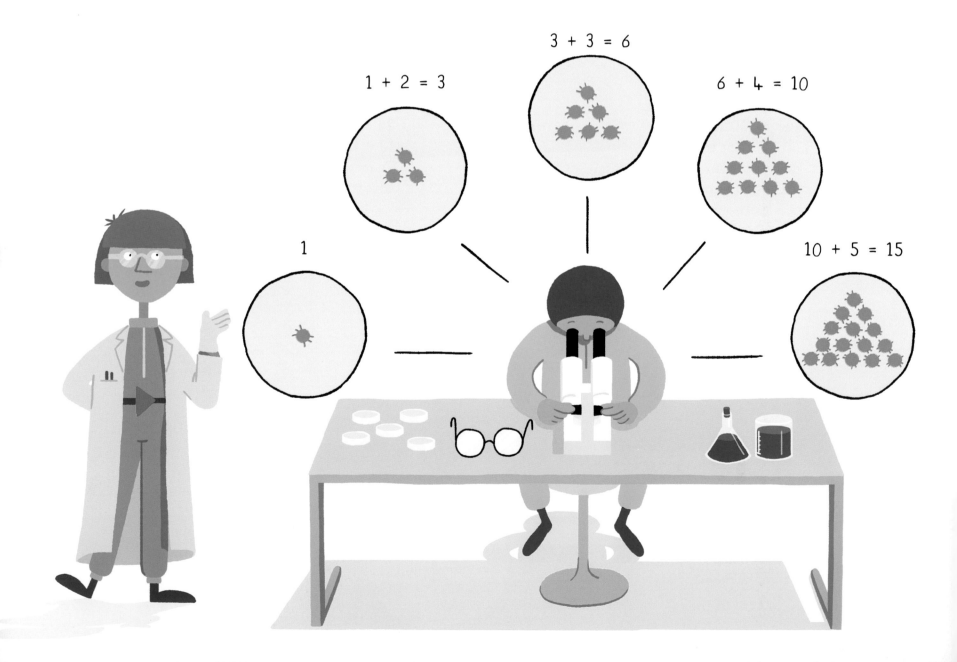

$1 + 2 = 3$

$3 + 3 = 6$

$6 + 4 = 10$

1

$10 + 5 = 15$

The Furballs are going to show you that triangular numbers can do some rather impressive things. **First of all, if you take one triangular number and add it to the next one, it makes a square number.**

Another remarkable fact is that **any number can be made by adding either two or three triangular numbers together.** Our old friend Carl Friedrich Gauss discovered this fact in 1796 when he was only 19 years old. **And a triangular number can never end in 2, 4, 7, or 9.** So don't even try it.

Triangular number + the next triangular number = square number!

3 + 6 = 9

10 + 15 = 25

ACTIVITY

In a game of pool, you start off with 15 balls arranged in a triangle. But in a game of interplanetary pool, we use many more balls: there are 10 balls along the base of the triangle. How many balls in total do we need for the game?

Tip: You need to figure out the 10th triangular number.

Answer: The tenth triangular number is 10 ÷ 2 × 11, which is 55.

What's the biggest number you can think of? Try to write it down. Chances are, there will be a lot of zeros after it, and writing it will take a long time! All those zeros seem to blur together, so it's hard to tell how big a long number actually is.

Instead of writing out huge numbers in full, we can use a system called powers of 10. If you want to write 1,000, but you can't be bothered to write the zeros out, you could write 10^3 instead. This means "10 to the power of 3." The little flying digit is the "power" and it tells you how many times to multiply the main number by itself. So 10^3 is a short way of writing $10 \times 10 \times 10$, or 1,000. Using this system, we can reach the dizzying heights of staggeringly large numbers pretty quickly. Ready? Buckle your seat belts!

10^1 m = 10 meters = Length of a bus
10^2 m = 100 meters = Length of a sprint track
10^3 m = 1,000 meters = Height of the world's tallest building
10^4 m = 10,000 meters = Height of the world's tallest mountain
10^5 m = 100,000 meters = Length of the Panama Canal
10^6 m = 1,000,000 meters = Length of the Rhine River
10^7 m = 10,000,000 meters = Circumference of the moon
10^8 m = 100,000,000 meters = ¼ of the way from Earth to the Moon
10^9 m = 1,000,000,000 meters = Width of the sun
10^{13} m = 10,000,000,000,000 meters = Width of the solar system
10^{21} m = 1,000,000,000,000,000,000,000 meters = Width of the galaxy!

TIP: DID YOU SPOT HOW THE NUMBER OF ZEROS IN EACH EXAMPLE IS THE SAME AS THE POWER DIGIT? THIS IS A HANDY TRICK TO REMEMBER. SO 10^{10} IS THE SAME AS A 1 FOLLOWED BY 10 ZEROS.

We can keep multiplying 10 by itself until eventually we get to a googol: a 1 followed by 100 zeros. And you can get numbers even bigger than that! A googolplex is a 1 followed by a googol of zeros. This makes a number that is too flabbergastingly enormous to write down. If a person can write two digits per second, then writing a googolplex would take about 1.51×10^{92} years, which is way, way greater than the age of the entire universe!

There's no limit to how big a number can be—they go on forever. Imagine of the highest number you can think of, then times it by 10 and keep going...to infinity and beyond!

GET READY FOR A BIG, BIG, BIG NUMBER...

How many tiny atoms do you think there are in the entire universe? A lot, right? Experts think that you can write this number as 10^{80}, which is one thousand quadrillion vigintillion atoms (yes, that's actually a real number).

ACTIVITY

To take off from planet Doris, we need 1,000,000 gallons of rocket fuel. But when Officer Denominator goes to the engine room, all the fuel-release buttons are labeled strangely! Can you help her decide which button to press?

A) 10^3 GALLONS
B) 10^4 GALLONS
C) 10^5 GALLONS
D) 10^6 GALLONS

Lesson 15
Fraction Action

Join me in the Cosmic Cafeteria, cadets—we're going to start splitting things into fractions, which are **parts of whole numbers.**

Four of my fellow crew members are sharing five pizzas. Easy, you say, they get one pizza each, with one pizza left over. They'll have to cut the remaining pizza into four equal slices, which are fractions of the whole.

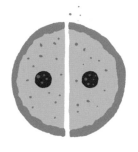

If you cut a pizza into two equal parts, each part is called a half, written $^1/_2$.

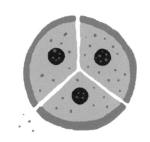

If you slice a pizza into three equal parts, each part is a third, written $^1/_3$.

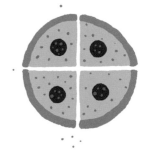

Slice it into four equal parts, and each part is called a quarter, written $^1/_4$.

With five equal parts, each part is called a fifth, written $^1/_5$.

As we've just seen, fractions can be written as one number on top of another, like this:

The **numerator** is the number on top. This tells us how many parts we're talking about.

The **denominator** is the number on the bottom. This tells us how many parts there are altogether. To remember which is which, just bear in mind that the **D**enominator is **D**own.

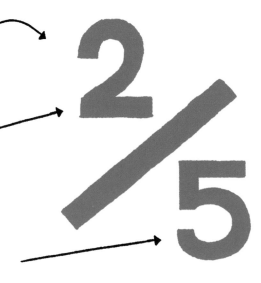

So $^2/_5$ means you have two parts out of a total of five parts. This Starbar has five equal parts. If we break off two of the parts, you'll see what $^2/_5$ looks like.

Please may I have $^1/_8$ of a Starbar?

I fancy $^6/_8$ of a Starbar, please.

I want $^8/_8$ of a Starbar!

If the number on top of the fraction is much smaller than the number underneath, then this means the fraction is quite small.

If the number on top is nearly as big as the number underneath, then this is quite a large fraction.

Watch out…if the number on top is **the same** as the number underneath, then this equals one whole—so greedy Adam Up is asking for **the whole** Starbar!

Take a look at these Starbars. You can see that $^1/_2$ a Starbar is actually the same size as $^2/_4$ of a Starbar, which is the same as $^3/_6$ of a bar. In fact, you can write the same amount in lots of different ways.

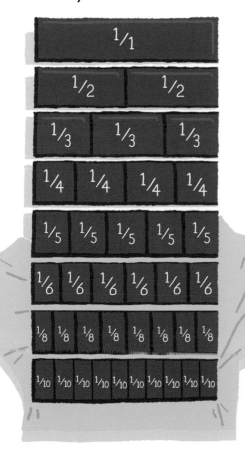

EASY FRACTIONS DISGUISED AS DIFFICULT FRACTIONS

The fraction $^6/_{18}$ seems a bit complicated. But we can easily zap it and turn it into a much friendlier-looking fraction. We just have to divide the top and the bottom by the same number. From our times tables, we know that both 6 and 18 can be divided by 6, so that's what we'll do.

$$\frac{6}{18} = \frac{6 \div 6}{18 \div 6} = \frac{1}{3}$$

So $^6/_{18}$ is actually the same as $^1/_3$. That's better!

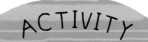

ACTIVITY

The Flurglewarpers choose their leader based on age. Bulbo is 487 $^3/_4$ and Gizmo is 487 $^3/_5$. Who is older?

Tip: If you need help, look at the Starbar chart to compare the sizes of quarters and fifths.

Answer: Bulbo is older, because $^3/_4$ is a bigger fraction than $^3/_5$.

Lesson 16
Delightful Decimals

We haven't finished with little bits of numbers yet, cadets! **Decimals are another way of writing parts of whole numbers.** Way back in Lesson 1, we learned about units, tens, and hundreds. Well, with decimals, we'll be dealing with tenths, hundredths, and thousandths. Take a look at this number:

HUNDREDS	TENS	UNITS		TENTHS	HUNDREDTHS	THOUSANDTHS
1	2	3	.	4	5	6

This dot is called a decimal point.

Just as we've seen before, the value of each number depends on its position. If a number is made up of digits to the left of the decimal point only, it is a whole number. All the digits on the right side of the decimal point are parts of numbers.

Units		Tenths	
1	.	1	1.1 is the same as 1 and $^1/_{10}$, so it's a tiny bit bigger than 1.
1	.	9	1.9 is the same as 1 and $^9/_{10}$, so it's almost equal to 2.
1	.	5	1.5 is the same as 1 and $^5/_{10}$, or $1^1/_2$, so it's right in the middle between 1 and 2.

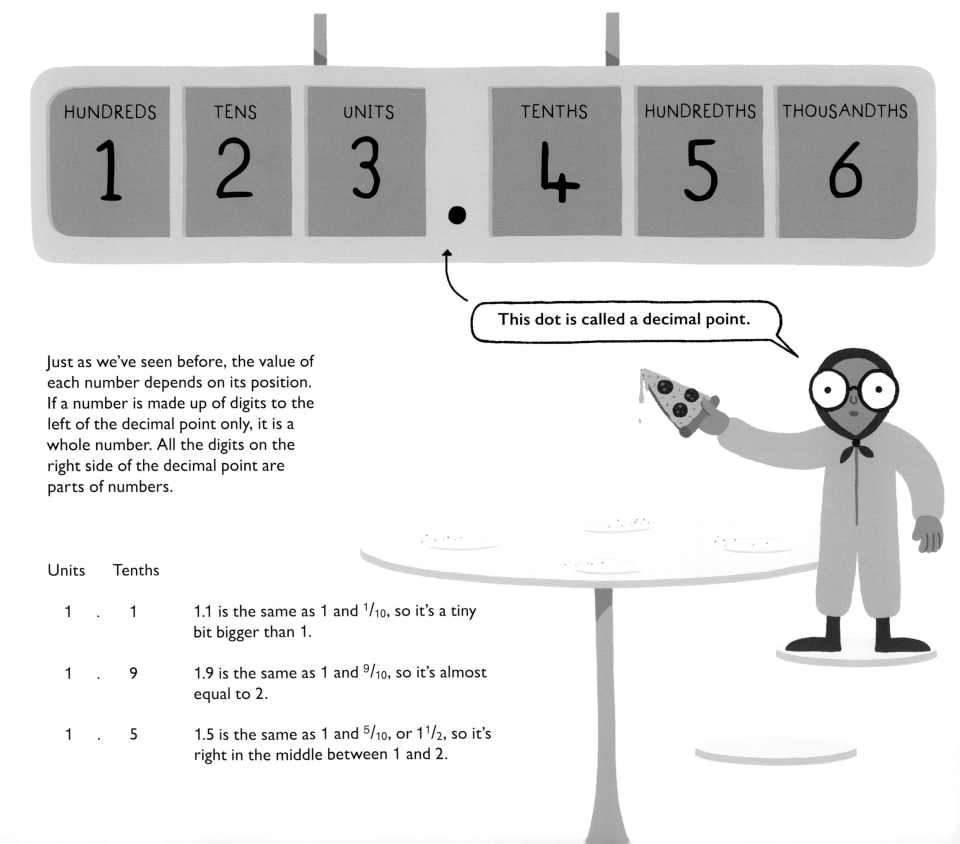

CALCULATOR TIP

It's easy to turn fractions into decimals using your calculator. Just divide the top number by the bottom number. To turn $1/4$ into a decimal, type in $1 \div 4$, which would give you the answer of 0.25.

DEADLY DECIMALS

Be warned, cadets: sometimes decimals can get very messy. If we try to divide 1 by 3, we could write this neatly as a fraction: $1/3$. But if you write it as a decimal it goes on forever: 0.3333333333…Sometimes it's easier to stick with fractions!

ACTIVITY

The Earth formed 4.5 billion years ago. Its surface was bombarded by asteroids until 3.9 billion years ago. For how many billion years did the asteroid bombardment last?

Tip: You can figure this out by doing a simple subtracting sum. Don't forget to line up the decimal points!

MONEY MATH

People use decimals all the time in everyday life. Take money, for example. $4.98 is four space zollars and 98 hundredths of a zollar. There are 100 zents in a zollar, so 98 hundredths of a zollar is the same as 98 zents. To add and subtract decimals, you do exactly the same as you would for adding and subtracting whole numbers. Just make sure the decimal points are lined up when you start. If you wanted to buy a Starbar, which costs $0.56, and a Squurgle Special Smoothie, which costs $2.40, how much will you need altogether?

Just do a normal adding sum—and don't forget to put a decimal point in your answer, lined up with the decimal points in the sum above. You'll need $2.96 altogether.

$$
\begin{array}{r}
0.56 \\
2.40 \\
\hline
2.96
\end{array}
$$

$2.50 $2.40

$0.56

The asteroid bombardment lasted for 0.6 billion years, because 4.5 minus 3.9 is 0.6.

$$
\begin{array}{r}
^3\!\!4.^15 \\
-3.9 \\
\hline
0.6
\end{array}
$$

(You can't do 5−9, so borrow one from the units column to give you 15.)

Lesson 17

What's a Percentage?

What's a percentage? I thought you'd never ask, cadets! **The word "percent" means "out of 100."** If we are faced by an invading fleet of 100 Black Hydra spacecraft, and 20 of them are bombers, then we'd say that 20 percent, or 20%, are bombers. **So percentages are another way of talking about parts of things, just like fractions and decimals.** Let's take a closer look at these pesky spacecraft.

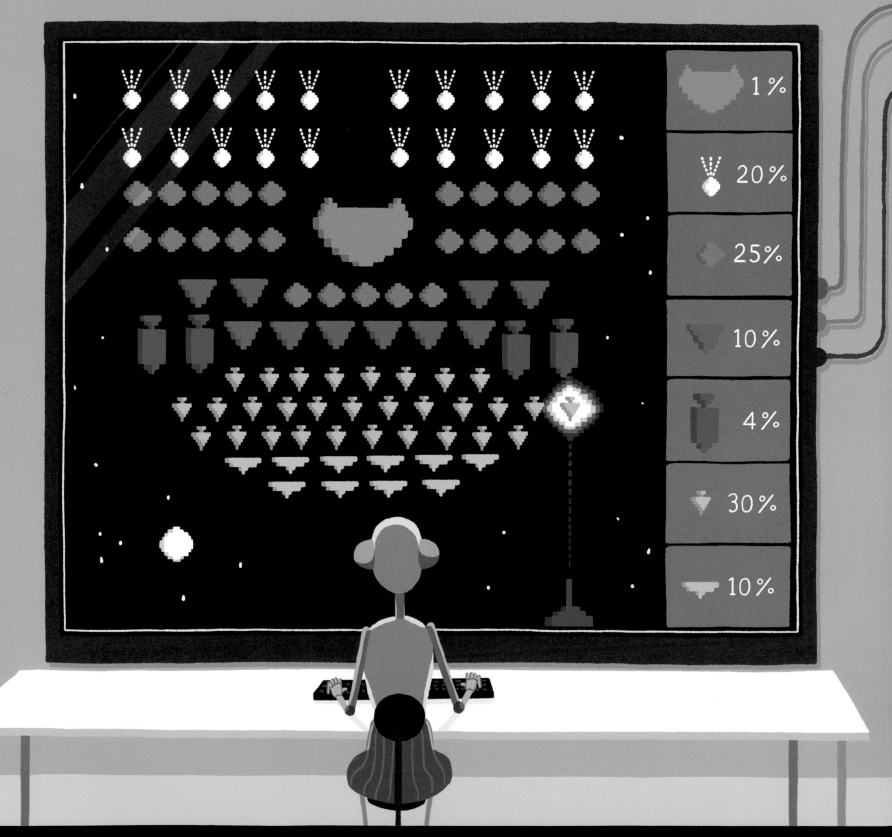

1%

20%

25%

10%

4%

30%

10%

Lois is going to show us her Amazing Convertor Machine. You feed in a fraction, and the machine instantly converts it into a decimal and a percentage. Here goes…

1/2	0.5	50%
1/4	0.25	25%
3/4	0.75	75%
1/5	0.2	20%
1/1	1	100%

It's really useful to remember these common conversions: knowing that 50% is the same as 0.5, which is the same as ½, is so useful, whether you're shopping in a sale or dividing up Starbars.

HOW DO YOU FIND A PERCENTAGE OF SOMETHING?

Sometimes, you might need to figure out a percentage. Imagine you're buying a uniform in the Alien Outfitters store, and there's a sale that gives you 20% off. If the original price is $300, how much will you save?

1. We need to take 20 percent off $300. To make things easier, it's useful to first figure out what one percent of $300 is. To do this, we simply divide by 100:

$300 ÷ 100 = $3

2. Now we know that one percent of $300 is $3, we just need to multiply this by 20 to find out what 20% is:

$3 x 20 = $60,

meaning that you will get $60 off your uniform. Lovely!

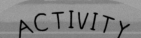

ACTIVITY

Planet Earth has an atmosphere made up of mainly nitrogen and oxygen, along with some other gases. If Earth's atmosphere is 78% nitrogen and 1% other gases, what percentage of the atmosphere is oxygen?

Tip: Remember, when dealing with percentages, that the total must add up to 100!

Answer: The Earth's atmosphere is 21% oxygen.

Lesson 18
Sequences and Series

Hi, gang. I'm in the middle of dealing with these Black Hydra spacecraft. Let's talk about number sequences, and then you can help me crack the Black Hydras' secret codes.

Often numbers form patterns called sequences, or series, which can go on and on and on. You've already seen a few sequences on your journey so far: times tables, square numbers, triangular numbers—they all have their own patterns. If you know the rule behind a pattern, you can figure out the next number, and the one after that—or any number in a series. So how do we crack the codes of these Hydras? **We need to look for the differences between the numbers to find out what the rule is.** Then we can use the rule to figure out the missing numbers.

| 16 | 22 | 28 | 34 | 40 | 46 | 52 | ? | ? |

In this sequence, the difference between each number is 6, so the next number will be 52 + 6, which is 58, and the one after that will be 58 + 6, which is 64. Sometimes, a sequence involves numbers being taken away instead of added; sometimes it might involve multiplication or division. But the method stays the same—**if you can figure out the rule, you can figure out the next number.**

ON THE DOUBLE

Legend has it that many years ago, the ruler of India loved playing chess so much that he wanted to give the game's inventor a reward. The wise inventor asked for one grain of rice on the first square of the chessboard, two grains on the second, four on the third, and so on, with the number doubling each time for all 62 squares. The ruler laughed, thinking this was a puny prize, and ordered his servants to bring the rice. But he was astonished when they told him that the total amount of rice would fill the entire palace—in fact, the pile would be bigger than Mount Everest! You can see that when you double numbers, they can grow massive pretty quickly...

1, 2, 4, 8, 16, 32, 64, 128, 256, 512, 1024, 2048, 4096, 8192...

Keep on completing the sequence if you like. How far can you get?

ACTIVITY

Can you figure out the missing numbers in these sequences to crack the Black Hydras' codes? If we can crack the codes, we can hack into their computer systems and disable their ships!
A) 25 50 75 100 125 ? ?
B) ? ? 24 21 18 15 12
C) 2 4 8 ? 32 64 ? 256
D) 640 320 160 80 ? ? 10

Lesson 19
The Fibonacci Sequence

Hello, my friends! You're back with your fearless leader to learn about a very important number series: the Fibonacci Sequence, which is named after the famous Italian mathematician Leonardo Fibonacci. In this sequence, every new number is the sum of the previous two numbers, so we have: 1, 1, 2, 3, 5, 8, 13, 21, 34, 55, 89, and so on.

FIBONACCI FLOWERS

Fibonacci numbers are all over the natural world. The next time you see a flower, check how many petals it has: the answer will probably be a Fibonacci number. Fibonacci numbers also appear in the patterns on sunflowers, pineapples, and cauliflowers. The middle of a sunflower has a pattern of spirals going clockwise and some going counterclockwise. If you count the two sets of spirals, they are always Fibonacci numbers—there are usually 21 and 34 spirals, or 34 and 55.

STRANGE BUT TRUE

Clovers usually have three leaves, and three is a Fibonacci number. Four-leaf clovers (not a Fibonacci number) are very rare indeed. Only about one clover in 10,000 has four leaves— that's why they're so hard to find.

THE GOLDEN RECTANGLE

Fibonacci numbers can be found not only in nature, but also in architecture. The ancient Greeks used a special type of rectangle when designing buildings because they thought it was particularly pleasing to look at. If you divide the length of the long side of a rectangle by the short side and get an answer of around 1.62, this means you have a golden rectangle. Golden rectangles are in all sorts of buildings, from ancient Greece's Parthenon to the Taj Mahal in India.

STRANGE SPIRALS

We can use Fibonacci numbers to make a spiral pattern. The first two numbers are both one, so we'll start off with two squares whose sides measure one unit each. Along one edge, we'll add another square, this time with sides measuring two units. Slowly we can add more squares, each one getting bigger and bigger, following the sequence. Then, if we trace a curve between the corners of each square, we'll make a spiral pattern. This is called the Golden Spiral, and you can find it not only in snail shells, but also in the spiral pattern of the Milky Way galaxy!

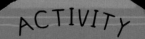

ACTIVITY

Look at the Fibonacci Sequence below. Can you figure out the next three numbers in the sequence?
I, I, 2, 3, 5, 8, 13, 21, 34, 55, 89

Answer: 144, 233, 377

Lesson 20
The Amazing Number 9

Welcome back, my friends! In this lesson, we're going to learn all about my favorite number: the mysterious number nine. Are you ready for a trick?

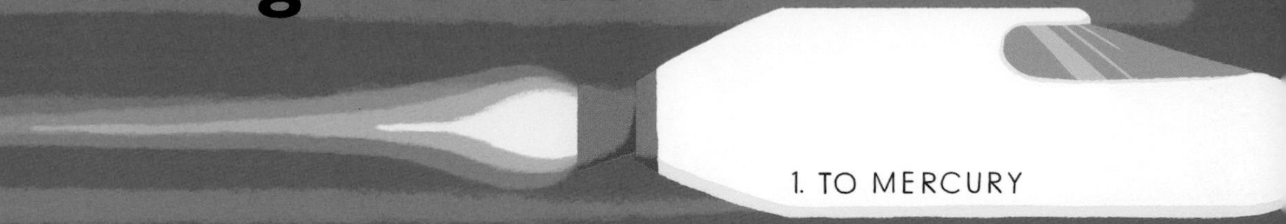

1 Start off by thinking of a number between one and nine.

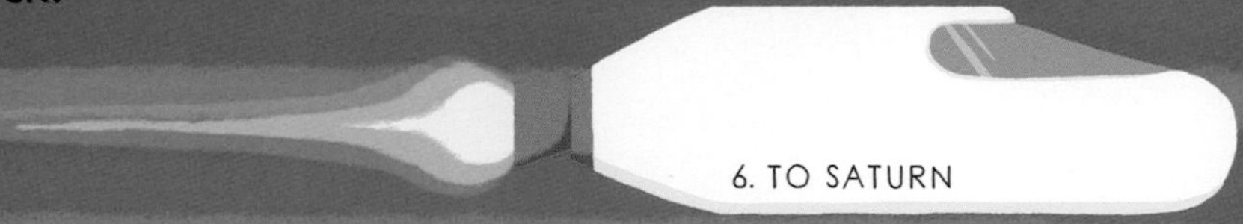

2 Next, multiply that number by nine.

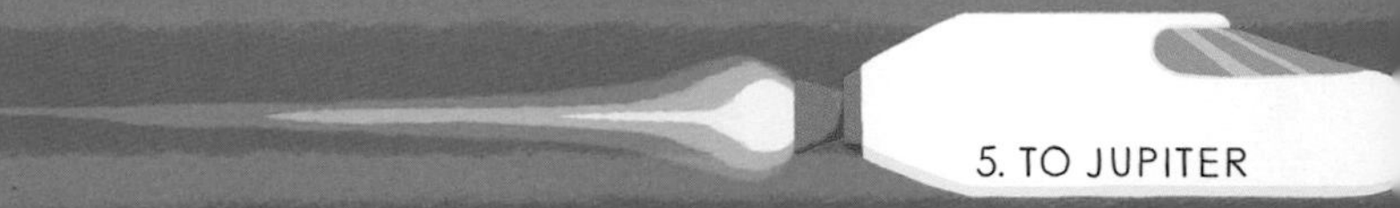

3 If the result has more than one digit, add those digits together. You should now be left with a single-digit number.

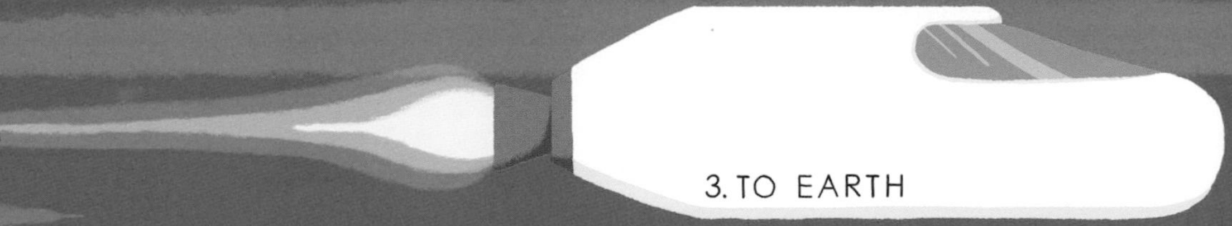

4 Now, take away five from the single-digit number to give you an answer.

5 Nine spacecraft are about to take off for different destinations. Does your answer match the number of any of the spacecraft shown here? Which planet are you heading for?

1. TO MERCURY

6. TO SATURN

5. TO JUPITER

3. TO EARTH

2. TO VENUS

7. TO URANUS

The moment of truth...I bet you're off to Mars! I'm not just a fantastic mind-reader: it's all in the math.

The key to this trick is in step 2, when you multiplied your number by nine. If you think back to Lesson 7, you might remember that when you add up the digits of **any number** in the nine times table, you always end up with nine (for example, $2 \times 9 = 18$, and $1 + 8 = 9$). So in step 3, when you added together the digits, I knew you'd be left with nine! The next few steps lead you straight into picking the Mars-bound spaceship. Sneaky, eh?

If you add up all the digits apart from nine, you get 36 (1 + 2 + 3 + 4 + 5 + 6 + 7 + 8 = 36). And if you add together the digits in 36 (3 + 6), you get nine!

MYSTERY MATH

If a number has three digits and you divide it by three nines, the number is turned into a repeating decimal. For example, 687 ÷ 999 = 0.687687687… Use a calculator to try this out. It works for any number, so long as you divide by an amount of nines that matches the number of digits in your original number.

Try this out on your fellow cadets. Ask them to write down a three-digit number (the digits should all be different), with the biggest first and the smallest last. Then get them to reverse the number and write it below—so the smallest digit is now in front. Ask them to take the bottom number away from the top number and write the answer down. Lastly, ask them to tell you what the **first** digit of their answer is. Once they've given you the first digit, you'll be able to tell them what their whole answer is!

So what's the secret? Whatever three-digit number you start with, the answer will **always** have a nine in the middle, and the first and third digits will **always** add up to nine. Let's try it out: imagine your friend chose the number 731. She would reverse it to get 137, then she'd take this away from 731 to leave 594. If she tells you that the first digit of her answer is a 5, you will be able to tell her that the answer is 594. Remember—the middle digit is always a 9, and the first and last digits have to add up to nine. Here, 5 + 4 = 9, so you know the last digit has to be a four. Give it a try!

4. TO MARS

8. TO NEPTUNE

9. TO OUTER SPACE

ACTIVITY

**Think of a number with two or more digits. Add the digits of the number together to give you an answer. Subtract the answer from your first number to give you another answer. Add the digits of that answer together. Keep adding the digits of your answer together until you come up with a single-digit number.
What is it?**

Answer: The single digit you end up with will always be…the number 9!

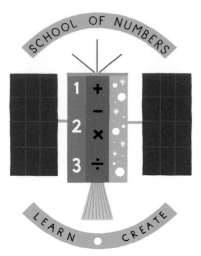

All Shapes and Sizes

Well done, cadets, you've made it to Term 2. By now, you should be feeling pretty comfortable playing around with numbers. But math isn't all about numbers. In Term 2, we'll discover the delights of geometry: the math of lines, shapes, and solids.

Geometry has been captivating and confusing humans for centuries. The word geometry comes from ancient Greek: *geo* for "Earth" and *metry* for "measurement." The ancient Greeks loved studying shapes, talking about shapes, drawing shapes in the sand, arguing about shapes…they got into some pretty heated debates, believe me. Later this term, we'll teach you a bit about the Greeks Euclid and Pythagoras: they were all-around geniuses and their teachings are still used today.

Understanding shapes is key to understanding the universe around us. Shapes and angles are everywhere—just take a look around the *Starship Infinity's* Control Room. From the circular buttons on the launch panel to the rectangular screens on every wall, from the triangular logos on our uniforms to the square tiles on the floor, the more you look, the more shapes you will discover. But what makes a triangle a triangle? What makes a circle a circle? Never fear, cadets, this term you will discover the secrets of shapes!

So why should we learn about shapes? There are so many practical uses for geometry. Our starship would never have been built if it weren't for the talented engineers who understood how to work the angles to make it safe and strong. Our rockets would never have taken off from Earth if it weren't for the clever designers who figured out the most streamlined shapes for blastoff. Have I convinced you yet? Let's shape up and ship out!

Lesson 21
Getting a Handle on Angles

Before we talk about shapes, we need to understand angles. Come with me to the starship's movie theater. We're not watching a film, though—we're on the hunt for Squigglehop antennae. If we slide in here behind this row of Squigglehops, we can take a look at their antennae, which are all at different angles. **When two straight lines meet, you get an angle between them.** Angles can be measured in degrees, which are written with a little floating circle, like this °. In a whole circle, or a full turn, there are 360 degrees, as we can see below. **An angle tells you the size of a turn.** If you start at the top, at 0°, and turn all the way around the circle, you've turned 360°.

Angles are given different names depending on how big they are. Which brings us back to our Squigglehops.

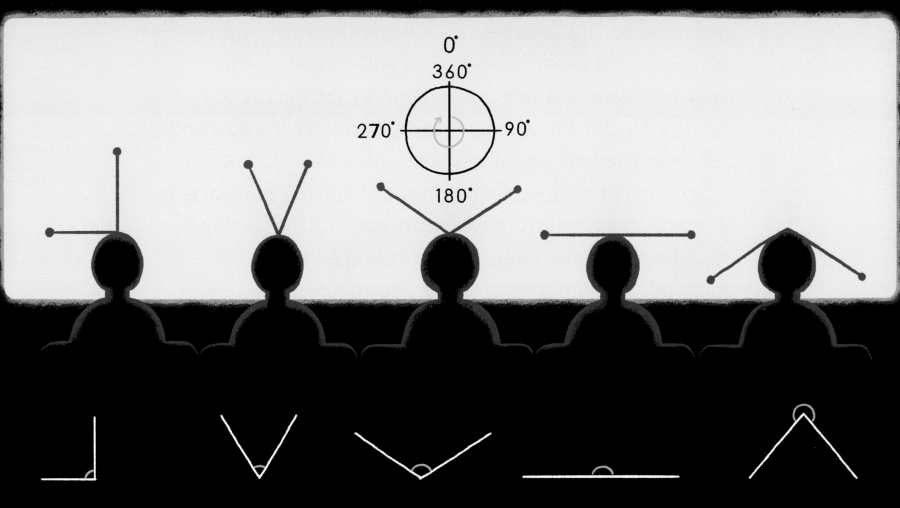

When the angle is exactly quarter of a circle, or 90°, it's called a **right angle.**

When an angle is quite small, less than 90°, it's called an **acute angle.**

If an angle is bigger than a right angle, but smaller than a straight line, it's called an **obtuse angle.**

If an angle is exactly 180°, or a half turn, then you've got a **straight line.**

And finally, if an angle is bigger than 180°, or more than half a turn, it's called a **reflex angle.**

ACTIVITY

To reach your next lesson, you have to meet Di in the Shuttle—but the route is full of twists and turns. Can you identify all the angles marked in yellow? Choose between an acute angle, an obtuse angle, a right angle, and a reflex angle. Some of them may crop up more than once…

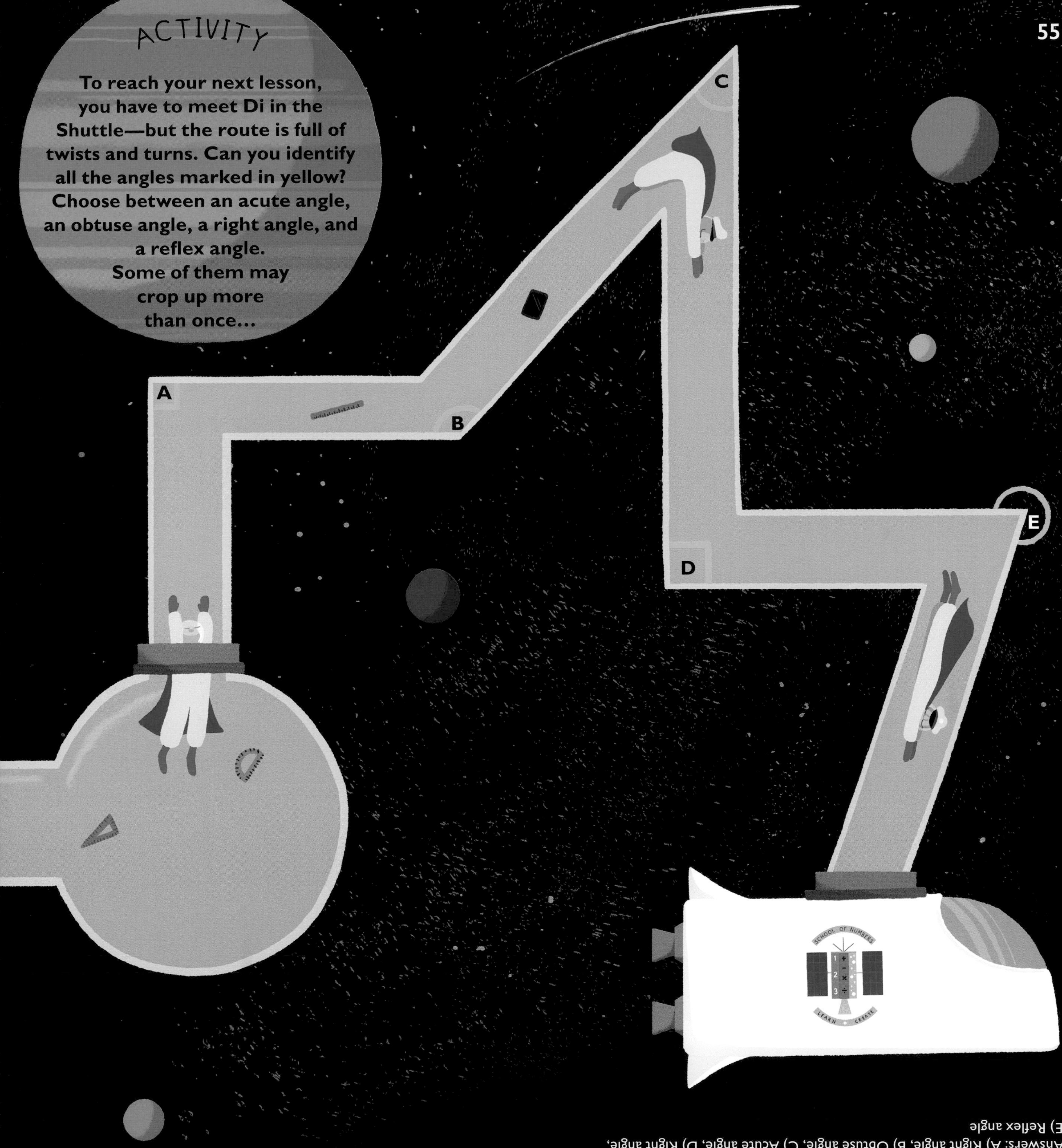

A

B

C

D

E

Answers: A) Right angle, B) Obtuse angle, C) Acute angle, D) Right angle, E) Reflex angle

Lesson 22
Ship Shapes

Hello, team. In this lesson, we're in the Space Dock to brush up on our shapes. But before we get down to the nitty gritty, let me tell you a bit about Euclid, who lived 2,300 years ago in ancient Greece. He was one the greatest mathematicians ever, and is known as the Father of Geometry. Most of what we know about shapes today comes from Euclid, who laid out rules for how particular shapes are made. Let's take a look...

MEET EUCLID

PARALLEL LINES

These are straight lines that are always the same distance apart. Even if they went on forever, they would never touch.

TIP

Did you know? A **quadrilateral** is the math name for any four-sided shape: squares, rectangles, trapezoids...you get the picture.

PUZZLING POLYGONS

A polygon is any shape made from straight lines: triangles, squares, rectangles, and hexagons are all polygons. **Regular polygons have equal angles and sides**, but irregular polygons are a bit more scruffy—their angles and sides aren't all equal.

SHAPING UP

The spaceships in our space dock all have different shapes. Can you match each spaceship to the description of its shape?

1. A **square** has four sides that are all the same length. Each of the corners is a right angle.

2. A **rectangle** has four sides, and the opposite sides are the same length. Each of the corners is a right angle.

3. A **circle** is a round shape with one curved edge that is always the same distance from the center.

4. An **equilateral triangle** has three equal sides and three equal angles.

5. An **isosceles triangle** has three sides, two of which are the same length.

6. A **scalene triangle** has three sides, all of which are different lengths.

7. A **rhombus** has four equal sides and no right angles. It's like a square that's been pushed over.

8. A **parallelogram** has four sides and no right angles. Its opposite sides are the same length and parallel. It's like a rectangle that's been pushed over.

9. A **trapezoid** has four sides and just one pair of parallel lines.

10. A **kite** has four sides: it has two equal short sides next to each other, and two equal long sides next to each other. There are no parallel sides.

11. A **pentagon** has five sides.

12. A **hexagon** has six sides.

13. A **heptagon** has seven sides.

14. An **octagon** has eight sides.

Terrific Triangles

The three sides are all different lengths.

All right, gang. We're going to have a closer look at the amazing world of triangles. It would be hard to pick a favorite shape, but if you pushed me, I'd go for the triangle. They're all around us—you can spot them on rooftops, bridges, road signs, and, of course, in sandwiches! Let's have a quick recap of the main types of triangle you might come across. The first three descriptions are based on the lengths of the three sides:

Equilateral triangle: All three sides are the same length.

Isosceles triangle: Two of the three sides are the same length.

These descriptions of triangles are based on the angles of each triangle. Sometimes, a triangle can match two descriptions. So, for example, an equilateral triangle is always, also, an acute triangle.

AN ISOSCELES TRIANGLE AND A SCALENE TRIANGLE CAN BOTH BE RIGHT-ANGLED TRIANGLES, BUT A RIGHT-ANGLED TRIANGLE CAN NEVER BE OBTUSE!

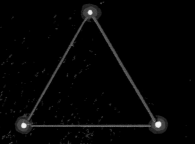

60°

60° 60°

Acute triangle: All the angles are smaller than 90°.

Right-angled triangle: One angle measures 90° exactly.

Obtuse triangle: One angle is greater than 90°.

ALL THE ANGLES MEASURE LESS THAN 90°, SO THIS EQUILATERAL TRIANGLE IS ACUTE.

PYTHAGORAS'S BIG IDEA

Pythagoras was an ancient Greek philosopher born about 2,600 years ago, who led a religious brotherhood that worshipped numbers. They believed that numbers had personalities, and thought that even numbers were female and odd numbers were male, apart from the number 1, which was the father and mother of all the other numbers! Pythagoras is most famous for his theory on triangles, which goes like this (brace yourselves): *For any right-angled triangle, the square of the hypotenuse is equal to the sum of the squares of the other two sides.*

Huh, I hear you say? Don't worry— we can draw an easy picture to explain what he meant:

$$9 + 16 = 25$$

25

9

16

The **hypotenuse** of a right-angled triangle is the longest side, and it's always opposite the right angle. What Pythagoras was getting at is this: if you draw a square along each edge of a right-angled triangle, the size of the big square will always be the same as the size of the two smaller squares added together. This simple piece of geometry has been used through the ages to help architects and engineers build pyramids, bridges, and skyscrapers. Thanks, Pythagoras!

KNOWING YOUR ANGLES

There's a simple rule to remember when it comes to triangles: **the three angles always add up to 180°.** And there's a neat way of showing this. Cut out a triangle and tear off the angles. Put all the angles together and you'll get a perfectly straight line. (And well done if you remember, from Lesson 21, that angles on a straight line always add up to 180°.)

180°

ACTIVITY

Make a right-angled triangle by cutting the corner off a piece of paper. Now tear off the two smaller angles. You'll be able to fit them perfectly into the right angle. This shows that on a right-angled triangle, the two smaller angles always add up to 90° exactly.

Lesson 24
Going Round in Circles

We're taking a field trip to the planet of Minotropia, where some strange circles have been left in the dust by an alien craft. Circles are very important shapes. Look around and you'll see circles everywhere—from the shapes and orbits of planets to the rings of a tree trunk. Technically, **a circle is a set of points that are all an equal distance from a central point.** Let me show you—if you draw enough points that are all the same distance from the center, you'll end up with a circle.

These points are all the same distance from the central dot.

There are various different parts
of a circle:

The **radius** is the distance
halfway across a circle.
Just think of a bike wheel:
the radius would be a
single spoke.

The **diameter** is the distance right
across the middle of a circle. It's
the same as two times the radius.

The **circumference**
is the distance
all the way around
a circle.

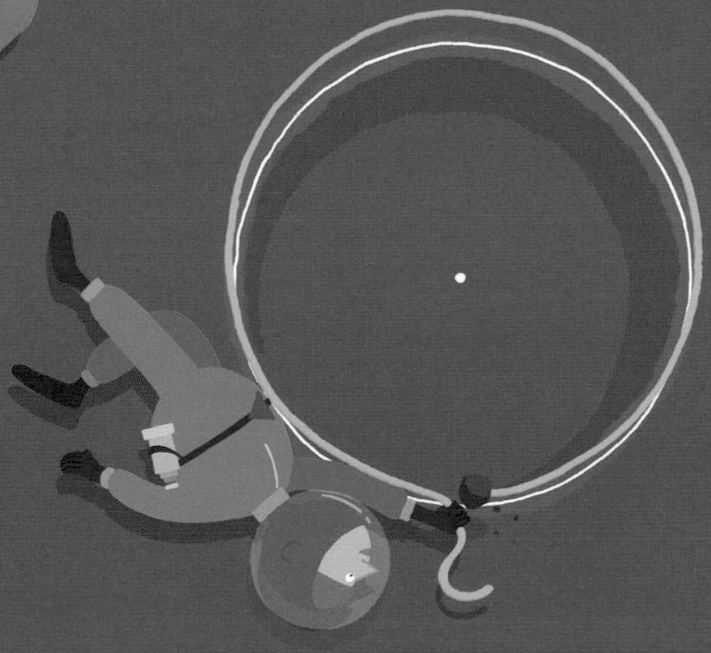

ACTIVITY

**If the radius
of planet Earth is
roughly 4,000 miles,
can you figure out
what Earth's
diameter is?**

Answer: Earth's diameter is roughly 8,000 miles,
because the diameter is 2 x the radius.

Lesson 25
Easy as Pi

Have you ever come across this little symbol: π? This symbol, which we call "pi," represents a number: probably the most famous number in the world (or the universe, for that matter).

If you divide the circumference of a circle by its diameter, you **always** get the same number, and we call this number pi. **Its value is about 3.14.**

STRANGE BUT TRUE

If you hold a mirror up to the number 3.14, it spells out PIE!

FINDING PI

1.
Try it for yourself. With a piece of string, go around the circumference of any circle you can find: it could be a Frisbee, a cup, a plate, or even an actual pie.

2.
Next, straighten the string out and measure it against a ruler, making a note of the answer.

3.
Then measure the circle's diameter with a ruler. Lastly, on a calculator, divide the circumference by the diameter.

4.
You should end up with a number very close to 3.14. Pi is a very useful number: if you know the diameter of any circle, you can figure out its circumference by multiplying the diameter by 3.14.

To keep things simple, we say pi's value is about 3.14, but it's actually much more complicated than this! The digits after the decimal point go on and on **forever**! One way of memorizing pi is to make up a useful phrase, then count the number of letters in each word of that phrase. So, for example, the question "May I have a large container of coffee?" would help you remember the first eight digits of pi (because "May" has three letters, "I" has one letter, "have" has four letters, and so on). Amazingly, in 2015, an Indian student named Rajveer Meena managed to recite 70,000 digits of pi from memory! It took him nearly 10 hours.

ACTIVITY

See how many digits of pi *you* can remember. Study the number here, then, when you're ready, ask a friend to test you.

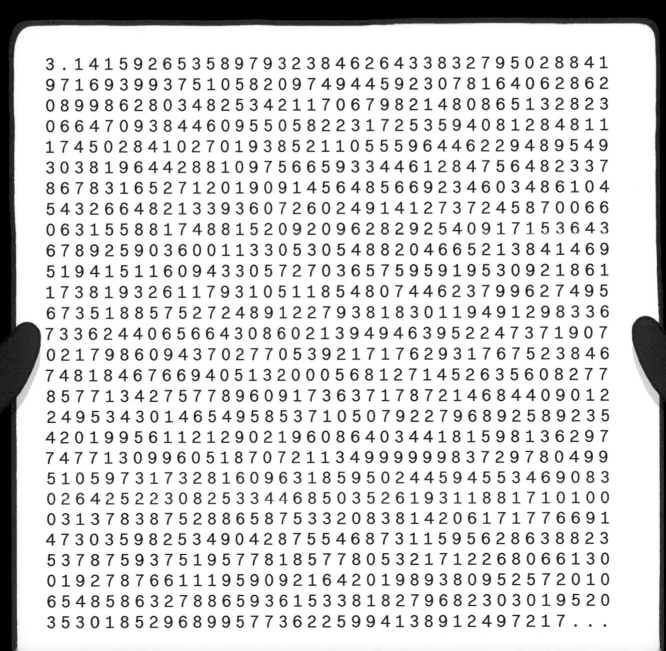

```
3.141592653589793238462643383279502884
19716939937510582097494459230781640628 62
08998628034825342117067982148086513282 3
06647093844609550582231725359408128481 1
17450284102701938521105559644622948954 9
30381964428810975665933446128475648233 7
86783165271201909145648566923460348610 4
54326648213393607260249141273724587006 6
06315588174881520920962829254091715364 3
67892590360011330530548820466521384146 9
51941511609433057270365759591953092186 1
17381932611793105118548074462379962749 5
67351885752724891227938183011949129833 6
73362440656643086021394946395224737190 7
02179860943702770539217176293176752384 6
74818467669405132000568127145263560827 7
85771342577896091736371787214684409012
24953430146549585371050792279689258923 5
42019956112129021960864034418159813629 7
74771309960518707211349999998372978049 9
51059731732816096318595024459455346908 3
02642522308253344685035261931188171010 0
03137838752886587533208381420617177669 1
47303598253490428755468731159562863882 3
53787593751957781857780532171226806613 0
01927876611195909216420198938095257201 0
65485863278865936153381827968230301952 0
35301852968995773622599413891249721 7...
```

Lesson 26
Puzzling Perimeters

Today we're touching down on the planet of Repton, where we're building a research base. We need to install a protective fence all the way around the base. Our challenge is to figure out how many feet of fencing we'll need.

To do this, we have to find the perimeter of the base. The perimeter is the distance all the way around the outside of a flat shape.

Let's make an X at one corner of the base. We'll go around from there,

measuring the length of every side. We'll know we've gone the whole way around when we get back to the X. Then we just need to add all the different lengths together.

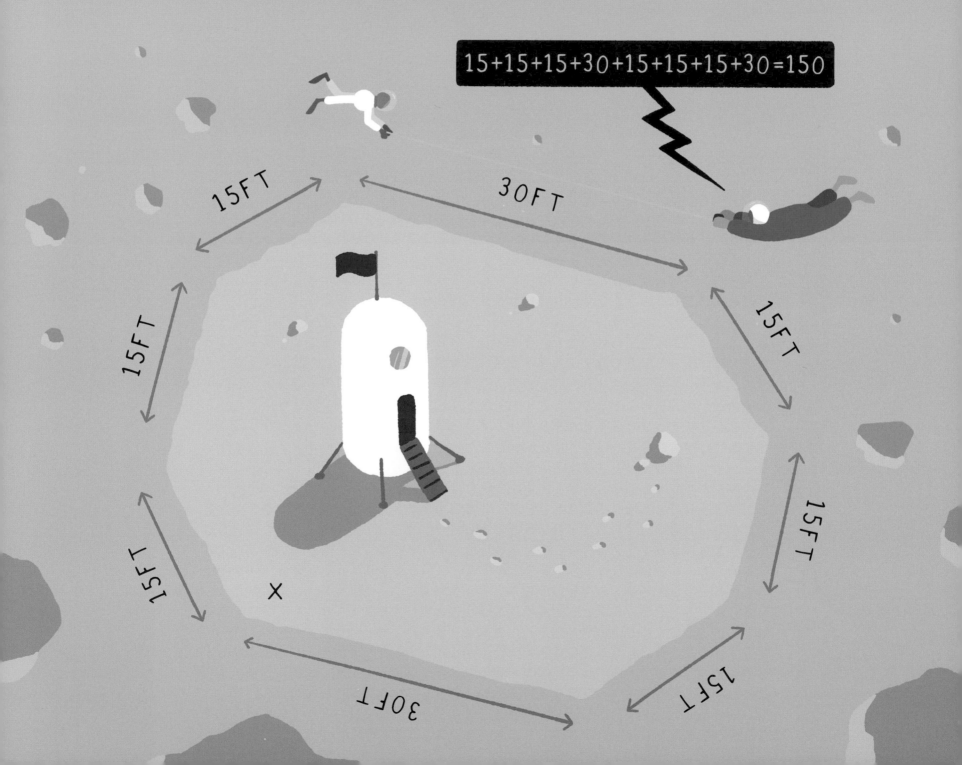

$$15+15+15+30+15+15+15+30=150$$

15FT

30FT

15FT

15FT

15FT

15FT

X

30FT

15FT

You might need to figure out a perimeter when you don't know the length of all the sides. Here's a sketch of a smaller camp that we need to build a fence for. The length of the longest side is missing from the sketch. But we can figure it out: the longest side is opposite a 12-foot and a 18-foot side. If you put these together, they would be the same length as the missing side, so you just add 12 + 18 feet, giving you 30 feet. Then we'll add an X as a starting point, and work our way around from there.

12 + 9 + 18 + 15 + 30 + 24 = 108 ft

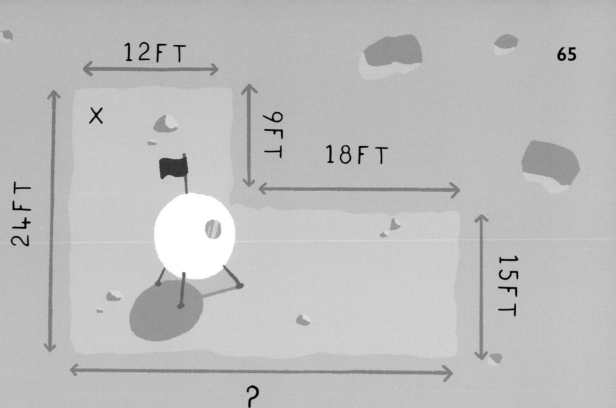

12 FT

9 FT

18 FT

15 FT

24 FT

X

?

110 YARDS

72 YARDS

?

?

ACTIVITY

Can you figure out the perimeter of the Intergalactic Soccer Field? Remember to figure out the lengths of the missing sides before you start.

Answer: The perimeter of the Intergalactic Soccer Field is 110 yards + 72 yards + 110 yards + 72 yards = 364 yards.

Lesson 27
Area Hysteria

Blistering blackholes, cadets, there you are at last! We've got a problem down here in the Investigation Station. We captured some radioactive Gammatroids for research, and we need to seal them inside lead-lined chambers to stop their harmful rays from getting out.

The chambers are ready, but we've forgotten the doors! We need to order some lead doors pronto—and to do that, we have to figure out the area of each doorway. This is important: **the area of a flat shape is the amount of space it takes up.**

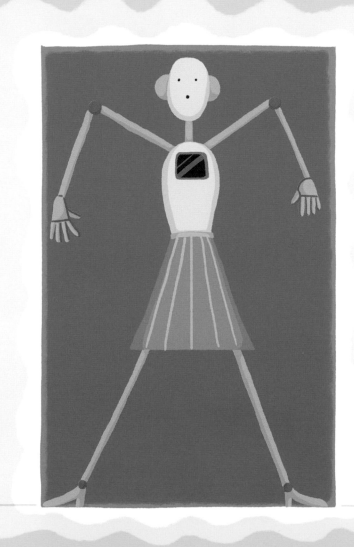

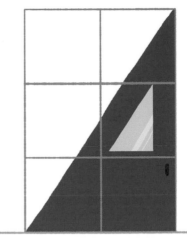

To find the area of a square or rectangle, you need to multiply width by height. So here, the area would be 1 foot × 3 feet, which equals 3…but 3 what, exactly? Feet? No, we measure area in squares, so the door needs to be 3 square feet.

We have a right-angled triangular doorway. **If you took two of these triangles and stuck them together, you'd get a rectangle.** The rectangle's area would be its width times its height, so the area of the triangle is half of this.
Rectangle's area = 3 feet × 2 feet = 6 square feet
Triangle's area = 6 feet ÷ 2 = 3 square feet

Circles are a bit trickier, but with the help of a calculator and our old friend pi, we should be able to manage. **The area of a circle can be figured out like this: radius × radius x pi (3.14).** In this case, the diameter of the circle is 5 feet, so the radius is half of this, or 2.5 feet.
Area of circular doorway = 2.5 feet × 2.5 feet × 3.14 = 19.625 square feet, which we can round to 20 square feet.

One of the Gammatroids has made a slimy puddle on the floor…Can you figure out the area of the puddle? Let's draw a grid over the slime, with each square having sides of 5 inches. The area of each square is 5 × 5 in = 25 square inches. We have to count the squares covered by slime. If more than half of a square is covered, we should count it. Here, there are 13 full squares and 9 squares that are more than half covered, giving us 22 squares altogether. Each square is 25 square inches, so the total area is 22 × 25, which is 550 square inches of slime. Yuck!

Lesson 28
Rock Solid:
The 3-D Shapes You Need to Know

Happy birthday, Captain Brown! We're having a little party for our leader, and it's a great chance to tell you all about solids. **Flat shapes have two dimensions (length and width), but solid shapes have three dimensions (length, width, and depth).** You can hold solid shapes in your hand: they all have faces, edges, and corners (which mathematicians call vertices). How many types of solid shape can you spot here? The sphere is the most important solid shape for astronomers: after all, the planets and stars are all spheres.

ACTIVITY

Can you spot a triangle-based pyramid? Make yourself sound really smart, and call this a tetrahedron!

Sphere

Cylinder

Cone

Triangular prism

Vertex

Face   Edge

A cube has 6 faces,
8 vertices, and 12 edges.

Cuboid

What a Transformation!

We all know that if you "transform" something, you change it. Shapes can be twisted, skewed, enlarged, and shrunk to become all sorts of different shapes—and these changes are called **transformations**.

TRANSLATION

If you slide a shape from one place to another, without changing how it looks, you're "translating" it. You can translate a shape by moving it up, down, left, or right. When we use our teleporter to beam each other up, this is translation!

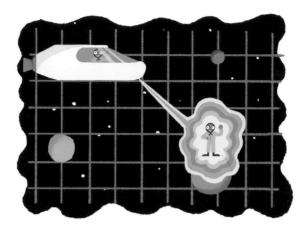

ROTATION

Another type of transformation is rotation, when a shape spins around a point. The point is called the center of rotation, and the shape can turn either clockwise or counterclockwise around it. Take a look at this spaceship, orbiting around a planet.

Center of rotation

ENLARGEMENT

If you enlarge a shape, you transform it by changing its size. To describe the change in size, we use something called a scale factor. If the scale factor is larger than one, the shape will get bigger. But, oddly, you can also make a shape smaller if you enlarge it with a scale factor of less than one. I'll demonstrate this on my colleagues, using my trusty laser gun. I'm going to enlarge Adam and Captain Brown by a scale factor of ½.

ACTIVITY

Adam is 85 inches tall, and Captain Brown is 60 inches tall. If I were to enlarge them both with a scale factor of 3, how tall will they be?

READY, BOYS?

THEY HAVE BEEN SHRUNK TO HALF THEIR PREVIOUS SIZE.

NOW I WILL ZAP THEM BACK TO NORMAL BY ENLARGING THEM WITH A SCALE FACTOR OF 2.

Answer: Adam will be 255 inches tall, and Captain Brown will be 180 inches tall.

Lesson 30
Symmetry and Tessellation

Phew. Now that I'm back to my normal size, we can get on with our next lesson. Today, we're going to learn about how shapes can fit together to make different patterns: this is called tessellation. But first, Lois is going to help me demonstrate symmetry.

SUPER SYMMETRY

A shape is symmetrical if you can draw a line across it so that each side of the line is a perfect mirror image of the other. Look at Lois—if I draw a line dividing her in half, we can see that both sides are exactly the same. She's symmetrical!

We call this line a **mirror line**, or a **line of symmetry**. The number of lines of symmetry a shape has is the same as the number of places you could position a mirror without changing the appearance of the shape. So, Lois has one line of symmetry...

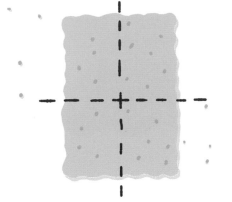

My morning toast has two lines of symmetry...

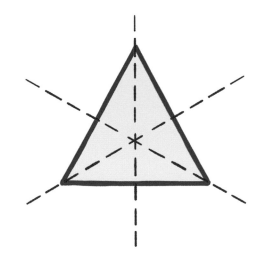

And the shape of the *Starship Infinity* logo (which is an **equilateral triangle**) has three lines of symmetry.

The reflection is the same distance away from the mirror line as the original.

Original   Reflection

Mirror line

A SECTION ON REFLECTION

Another type of transformation is reflection, where a shape is flipped to give a mirror image. When you look in a mirror, your reflection appears exactly the same distance behind the mirror as you are in front of it. And it's the same with everything else: when a shape is reflected, its reflection will be exactly the same distance away from the mirror line.

NEXT STOP: THE TESSELLATION STATION

A shape will tessellate if it can slot together with other identical shapes leaving no gaps, with no overlaps.
The only regular shapes that tessellate perfectly are equilateral triangles, squares, and hexagons.

GENIUS BEES

Bees store their honey in a pattern of tessellating wax hexagons. But why do they go for hexagons? The answer is that hexagon-shaped cells hold more honey and take less wax to build than cells of any other shape. For example, if a bee built a triangular honeycomb, she would need to build six walls at every point where the triangles meet. But with hexagons, our clever bee only needs to build three walls at each junction—meaning less time building, and more time making honey!

SPACE
DOCK

ACTIVITY

Turn the words on the left upside down and look at them in a mirror. What happens? The word "SPACE" looks jumbled up but the word "DOCK" appears normal. Why? "DOCK" is made up of letters that have horizontal symmetry, which means that if you draw a line exactly through the middle, horizontally, the two halves of the word perfectly reflect each other. Can you think of any other words that have horizontal symmetry?

Term 3

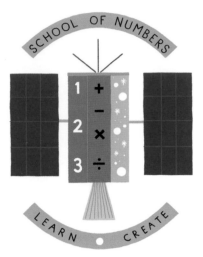

Real-World Math

Good work, cadets—you've made it to your final term. Now we're going one step further and exploring how you can make use of math in your daily lives. You'll discover how to master measurements and maps, and how to grapple with graphs and statistics. We'll also use math to delve into astronomy, which will help you aboard the *Starship Infinity*.

We use math in our everyday lives without even realizing it. To figure out how to get somewhere on time, you use math. If you want to figure out which packet of Starbars is the best value, you need math. We use math to solve many real-world problems, from designing vehicles, to figuring out the amount of fuel needed for a trip to the moon. Even baking is math!

One important part of real-world math is the math of measurement. Nowadays, we take measurements like the foot (for length) and the minute (for time) for granted. But have you ever wondered how measurements came about? Or imagined what the world would be like without them? For a start, you couldn't have a party, because people wouldn't know what time to arrive. Cooking would be difficult, because you wouldn't know how much of each ingredient to use. Even buying clothes would be tricky—without set sizes! And humans would never have made it to space without detailed measurements. Find out more about marvelous measurements later this term.

Did you know that, in a room of just 23 people, there's a 50 percent chance that two of them have the same birthday? This is all to do with probability, the math of chance, which we'll also be tackling this term. You might already have an idea what the word "average" means, but did you know that in math, there are three different types of average, called the mean, median, and mode? You'll meet these useful terms in our lesson on statistics—the math of data.

By the time you've reached the end of Term 3, you'll look at the world, and the universe for that matter, in a whole new light, seeing mathematics everywhere. Let's lift off and explore a whole galaxy of math!

Lesson 31
Body Math

Jump to it, cadets! In this lesson, we're going to reveal how math is all around us, including in places we're not expecting to find it. Even our bodies are arranged according to certain mathematical rules! People come in all shapes and sizes—little and large, short and tall. But we're actually more similar than you might think. Although our bodies are all different sizes, the proportions of our bodies are often very similar.

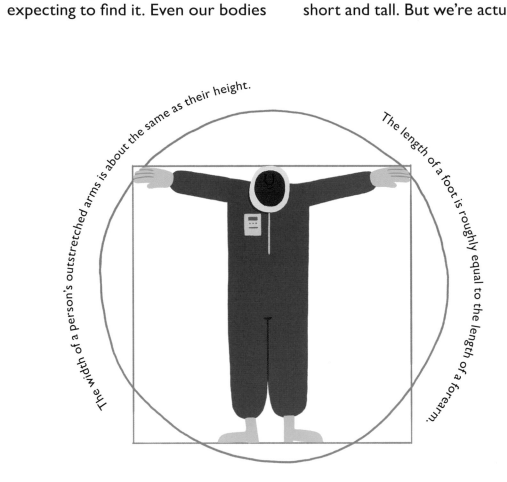

The width of a person's outstretched arms is about the same as their height.

The length of a foot is roughly equal to the length of a forearm.

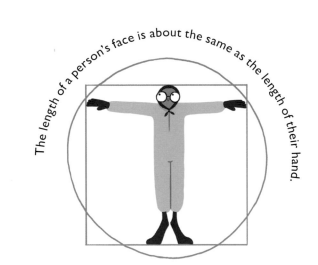

The length of a person's face is about the same as the length of their hand.

Lois and Adam are very different in size, but you can see that each of them is about seven heads tall when standing straight. The same is true for many adults. Babies have huge heads in relation to the size of their bodies—they need big brains because there's so much to learn. As people grow, their arms, legs, and bodies stretch out, but the head doesn't grow much bigger.

MIRROR, MIRROR

There are some general rules that apply to our faces, too. Your eyes are separated by a distance of about one eye width, and they are about halfway between the top of your head and your chin. And on most people, ears start in line with the top of the nose and finish in line with the bottom of the nose. Look in the mirror and see for yourself!

LOOKING GOOD TODAY, AL!

Lesson 32
Mastering Measurements

Measurements allow us to compare the quantities and sizes of different things. Long ago, people measured things using their body parts. This is where the terms "feet" and "yards" come from. But not everyone's feet were the same size, leading to lots of disagreements! The ancient Egyptians were some of the first to standardize measurements. They created a royal cubit, which was the distance from the pharaoah's elbow to the tip of his middle finger. Granite cubits were sent across the country, which helped the Egyptians create amazing buildings. The blocks of the pyramids were all measured with a cubit rod, so they were all a uniform size. But most measurements only applied to a certain region, so traveling and trading were difficult.

Yard: From the tip of the nose to the end of the thumb

Fathom: The space between the outstreched arms

Hand: The width of the hand (including the thumb)

Cubit: From the point of the elbow to the tip of the middle finger

Thumb: The thickest width of the thumb

THE MARVELOUS METER

The French Academy of Sciences decided to create a measurement for length based on something universal and unchanging—Earth. And so the meter was born: a length that was one ten-millionth of the distance from the North Pole to the Equator. The official meter bar was made from platinum in 1799, and copies were sent all over the world. The meter became the international unit for length.

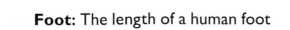

Foot: The length of a human foot

SI UNITS

The SI system (which stands for the French *Système International*) is the most widely used system for measuring things. There are seven different units, each for measuring something different.

WHAT IS BEING MEASURED?	UNIT	ABBREVIATION
LENGTH	METER	M
TIME	SECOND	S
TEMPERATURE	KELVIN	K
MASS (WEIGHT)	KILOGRAM	KG
BRIGHTNESS	CANDELA	CD
AMOUNT OF ELECTRICAL CURRENT	AMPERE	A
AMOUNT OF CHEMICAL SUBSTANCE	MOLE	MOL

HOW BIG IS A UNIT?

We can stick a prefix on the beginning of a unit of measurement if we need to make the unit bigger or smaller. For example, the prefix "kilo" multiplies the unit by one thousand, so a "kilometer" means 1,000 meters. Here are the most popular prefixes:

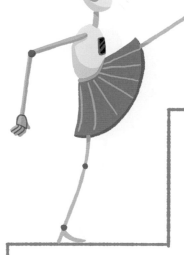

Giga: Multiplies the unit by one billion, or a thousand million (so there are 1 billion years in a gigayear)

Mega: Multiplies the unit by one million (so, in computing, there are 1 million bytes of information in a megabyte)

Kilo: Multiplies the unit by one thousand (there are 1,000 meters in a kilometer)

Centi: Divides the unit by one hundred (there are 100 centimeters in a meter)

Milli: Divides the unit by one thousand (there are 1,000 millimeters in a meter)

MEASUREMENT MIX-UPS

In many places, including the U.S., people use different systems of measurement, including feet and inches for height, which are called "imperial" measurements. In 1999, NASA lost a Mars orbiter worth $125 million, because one of the engineering teams used imperial measurements, while another team used SI units. Whoops!

ACTIVITY

Can you figure out these conversions?
1. **What is 0.08 meters in centimeters?**
2. **What is 4,000 meters in kilometers?**
3. **What is 0.009 meters in millimeters?**

Answers: 1. 8 centimeters, 2. 4 kilometers, 3. 9 millimeters

Lesson 33
Distances in Space

Distances in space are mind-bogglingly big, so we need measurements bigger than the humble meter to deal with them. The solar system is the name for the sun and the eight planets (including Earth) that go around it. To understand the size of the solar system, it's useful to think first about the size of Earth. If you were to drive nonstop right through the middle of the Earth, and out the other side, it would take about a week. That seems pretty big! But now, imagine Earth was the size of a grape. If the Earth were a grape, the sun would be the size of a giant beach ball 500 feet away. And the farthest planet, Neptune, would be the size of a tennis ball, about 50 soccer fields away. To drive to Neptune, it would take about 7,000 years! If you imagine the whole solar system is like a tiny grain of sand compared to the enormity of the Milky Way and the universe, you'll see why astronomers need some hefty measurements to deal with all these distances. So allow me to present the astronomical unit, the light-year, and the parsec…

MERCURY

THE ASTRONOMICAL UNIT (FOR SPACE THINGS THAT ARE PRETTY CLOSE)

We use astronomical units (AU) to measure distances in the Earth's solar system. **One AU is the average distance between the Sun and Earth, which is about 93 million miles.** It would take an airliner more than 20 years to fly that distance. The planet Saturn is 10 AU from the sun, which means it is ten times farther away from the sun than Earth is.

IF EARTH WERE THE SIZE OF A GRAPE, NEPTUNE WOULD BE 50 SOCCER FIELDS AWAY!

NEPTUNE

URANUS

SATURN

JUPITER

MARS

EARTH

VENUS

THE PARSEC (FOR SPACE THINGS THAT ARE REALLY, REALLY FAR AWAY)

For really massive distances in space, such as the distances between galaxies, astronomers use a unit of measurement called the parsec. The parsec is equal to 3.26 light-years. For even bigger distances, they use the kiloparsec (one thousand parsecs) and the megaparsec (one million parsecs). The Milky Way galaxy is roughly 34 kiloparsecs across, which is the same as about 110,000 light-years.

THE LIGHT-YEAR (FOR SPACE THINGS THAT ARE FAR AWAY)

A light-year is the distance a ray of light travels in a whole year. Light travels very quickly: if you could run at the speed of light, you could circle the Earth more than 7 times in a single second.
A light-year is about 6 **trillion** (6,000,000,000,000) miles. The closest star to Earth's sun is called Proxima Centauri, and it is 4.3 light-years away (more than 25 trillion miles).

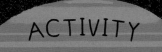

ACTIVITY

The Andromeda galaxy is ¾ megaparsecs from the Milky Way galaxy. If the Sombrero galaxy is 11¼ megaparsecs farther away than the Andromeda galaxy, how far away (in megaparsecs) from the Milky Way galaxy is it?

Answer: The Sombrero galaxy is 12 megaparsecs away from the Milky Way (¾ mps + 11¼ mps).

Lesson 34
Keeping Time

Before watches and clocks were invented, measuring time was tricky. The clever ancient Egyptians came up with a way of telling the time: the sundial. But the sundial had its drawbacks: it didn't work on a cloudy day, or at night!

The first mechanical clocks were invented in the 14th century, but people had to rely on the sun to set them, when it was directly overhead at noon every day. This meant that one town's 12 noon was slightly different to its neighbor's. When railways arrived in England, this caused lots of problems: people had to reset their watches at every station! And so, "Railway Time" was introduced—one standard time across the whole of the UK.

WHY ARE THERE 60 MINUTES IN AN HOUR?

There are 24 hours in a day, 60 minutes in an hour, and 60 seconds in a minute. But why? This system comes from the ancient Babylonian people, who lived 4,000 years ago. They counted in groups of 60, instead of in groups of 10 like we do today. The number 60 is useful for timekeeping, because it can be easily divided into smaller chunks (of 5 minutes, 10 minutes, 15 minutes, and so on).

ANALOG TIME

With analog time, we split the 24-hour day in half. The first 12 hours of a day, from midnight to midday, are called "a.m." (from the Latin words *ante meridiem*, meaning "before midday").

The next 12 hours, from midday to midnight, are called "p.m." (from the Latin *post meridiem*, or "past midday"). At 8 a.m. you may be eating your breakfast, but at 8 p.m. you're probably on your way to bed.

DIGITAL TIME

With digital time, we count each of the 24 hours in every day. So after 12:00 midday, the clock numbers continue to increase: 1 p.m. becomes 13:00, 2 p.m. becomes 14:00, and so on. At midnight, the clock resets to 00:00, before starting all over again.

Hours

Minutes

Seconds

`15:30:45`

DIGITAL

ANALOG

STRANGE BUT TRUE

In France in 1793, a decree was signed stating that every day would be divided into 10 hours, with each hour divided into 100 minutes, and each minute divided into 100 seconds. The new system didn't catch on.

ACTIVITY

We run the *Starship Infinity* using digital times, but my assistant has used analog times on my daily schedule by mistake. Can you convert them to digital times, using the 24-hour clock?
1) Morning briefing: 8:30 a.m.
2) Lunch with Lois: 12:30 p.m.
3) Meeting with Captain to discuss Black Hydra threat: 4 p.m.
4) Intergalactic soccer match (friendly): 7:30 p.m.

Answers: 1. 08:30, 2. 12:30, 3. 16:00, 4. 19:30

Lesson 35
The Need for Speed

Today, we're going to be learning all about speed: how fast something is traveling. Speeds are often given in "feet per second" or "miles per hour." But what, in heaven's name, does "per" mean? It simply means "for each." A cheetah can run at 95 feet per second, which means that for each second it runs, it covers 95 feet. Pretty speedy!

To figure out speed, you need to know two things: the distance covered and the time it takes to travel that distance. Here's the important bit: **speed is the distance you move divided by the time it takes, so Speed = Distance ÷ Time.** The crew are going to have a race. Who do you think will win? Easy! We just look at which spaceship has

the fastest speed. But how do we know which is fastest? How do miles per hour stack up next to feet per second? How do you compare inches per minute with miles per minute? We need to choose one type of speed, and switch all the others to match it. Let's go for miles per hour.

Ava is flying a Space Zoomer with a top speed of 2 miles per minute.

Al has commandeered a Black Hydra Cruiser with a top speed of 460 miles per hour.

Di is racing in a Gammatroid Interceptor, with a top speed of 195 feet per second.

Al's speed is already in miles per hour, so we don't have to convert it. The top speed is 460 miles per hour.

We need to change Ava's speed of 2 miles per minute into miles per hour. There are 60 minutes in an hour, so however far we travel in a minute, we will travel 60 times as far in an hour. So, we need to multiply 2 miles by 60, giving us 120 miles per hour.

Next is Di's Gammatroid Interceptor. We must convert 195 feet per second into miles per hour. We will travel much farther in an hour than a second, so we need to multiply.

There are 60 seconds in a minute and 60 minutes in an hour, so that gives us $60 \times 60 = 3,600$ seconds in an hour. If the Interceptor does 195 feet in one second, then in an hour it does 195 feet $\times$ 3,600 seconds = 702,000 feet per hour.

How do we convert feet per hour into miles per hour? There are 5,280 feet in a mile, so we will travel fewer miles than feet: we need to divide. We can convert 702,000 feet per hour to miles per hour by dividing by 5,280, which equals about 133. Voila! The Interceptor travels at 133 miles per hour.

Next comes Adam in his Blophopper, which has a speed of 100 inches per minute. To find out how many inches per hour he travels, we multiply 100 by 60 (because there are 60 minutes in an hour). So $100 \times 60 = 6,000$ inches per hour.

How many miles per hour is this? There are 12 inches in a foot, and 5,280 feet in a mile, so there are $12 \times 5,280$ inches in a mile, which makes 63,360. Now we need to divide 6,000 by 63,360 to give us an answer of 0.09 miles per hour. Poor Adam. Walking would be quicker!

Adam is flying an Octophant Blophopper, with a top speed of 100 inches per minute.

Captain Brown is racing in an Intergalactic Defender with a top speed of 300 feet per second.

Answer: The Captain's Intergalactic Defender travels at 205 miles per hour. Al Jabra will be the winner, because his speed of 460 miles per hour is the fastest.

Lesson 36

What Are Statistics?

I'm going to teach you all about my favorite type of math: statistics. Statistics is the study of data: how to collect it, and how to present it. If you are faced with lots of numbers—aliens' heights, crewmembers' shoe sizes, or spaceship speeds—a knowledge of statistics will help you sort them out and understand them. I find it ever so soothing!

FINDING THE AVERAGE

One of the most important ideas in statistics is the **average**: a single number that represents a *typical* value in a group of numbers. There are three different types of average: the **mean**, **median**, and **mode**. Let's take a look at the moons of the solar system. We're going to include Pluto as a planet (even though it's officially a dwarf planet). This will make it easier for us to figure out the median—you'll see why later. Each planet has its number of moons written below it.

MERCURY	VENUS	EARTH	MARS
0	0	1	2

To find the **mean** of a group of numbers, you add all the numbers together, then divide by the total number of values. So here, you'd add up the number of moons and divide by the number of planets.

0 + 0 + 1 + 2 + 69 + 62 + 27 + 14 + 5 = 180 moons
180 ÷ 9 planets = 20

The mean number of moons is 20.

To find the **median**, you arrange the numbers in size order, then find the one in the middle. Here are the numbers of moons arranged in size order:
0   0   1   2   5   14   27   62   69
The median number of moons is 5, because it is the number in the middle. (Now you can see why it was helpful to include Pluto—finding the middle number is easier if there are an odd number of values.)

If you have an even number of values, there are **two** middle numbers. To find the median, you must figure out the **mean** of the two middle numbers.

To find the **mode**, you simply take the value that appears the most times in a group of numbers. With this group of moons, the mode is actually 0, because it is the only number that appears more than once.

The average number of moons in the solar system can be either 20, 5, or 0, depending which type of average you use! Although the mean is a very useful tool for finding an average, you need to be slightly cautious. If there are a few values that are much higher or lower than the rest of the group, the mean can become skewed. Jupiter and Saturn have lots of moons compared with the other planets, so these high numbers drag the mean upward. Here I'd say that the median actually gives you a better idea of a typical number of moons.

JUPITER

SATURN

URANUS

NEPTUNE

PLUTO

69

62

27

14

5

ACTIVITY

As a crew, we all have very different shoe sizes: Adam is a size 14, Captain Brown wears a size 10, Di is a size 4, Lois is a size 5, Al Jabra wears a size 9, and I wear a size 6. Can you figure out the mean of our shoe sizes?

Answer: The mean shoe size is 48 ÷ 6 = 8.

Lesson 37
Graphs and Charts

Graphs and charts are really useful because they show information visually so you can compare things without having to look at lots of numbers. There are all sorts of different types of graphs...

BAR CHARTS

These handy charts have different length bars to represent different values. This bar chart shows the desserts sold in the Cosmic Cafeteria on Tuesday:

PICTOGRAMS

With a pictogram, you don't even need the numbers up the side. Instead, images are used to represent numbers. Here, you can see which activity was most popular on board the *Starship Infinity* last Wednesday evening.

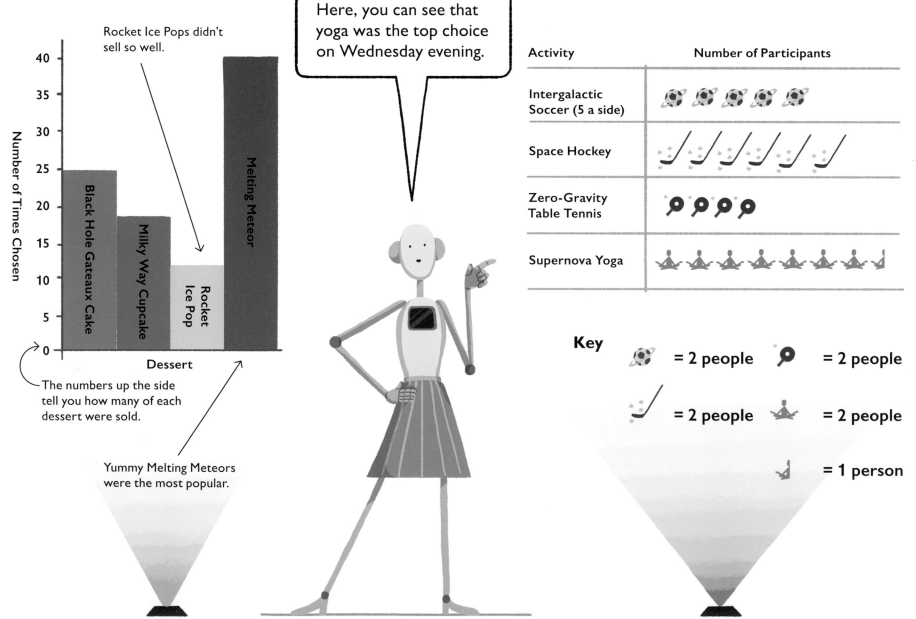

Rocket Ice Pops didn't sell so well.

Here, you can see that yoga was the top choice on Wednesday evening.

Number of Times Chosen

Black Hole Gateaux Cake

Milky Way Cupcake

Rocket Ice Pop

Melting Meteor

Dessert

The numbers up the side tell you how many of each dessert were sold.

Yummy Melting Meteors were the most popular.

Activity	Number of Participants
Intergalactic Soccer (5 a side)	
Space Hockey	
Zero-Gravity Table Tennis	
Supernova Yoga	

Key

= 2 people   = 2 people

= 2 people   = 2 people

= 1 person

LINE GRAPHS

A line graph is similar to a bar chart, but the line cuts across where the tops of the bars would go. This line graph shows the speed of Captain's Brown's Starship Rover as it races down the corridor.

Pie charts have different-sized sections representing different things. They are useful for showing proportions. This pie chart shows the makeup of the latest Intergalactic Council Meeting, which 12 members attended.

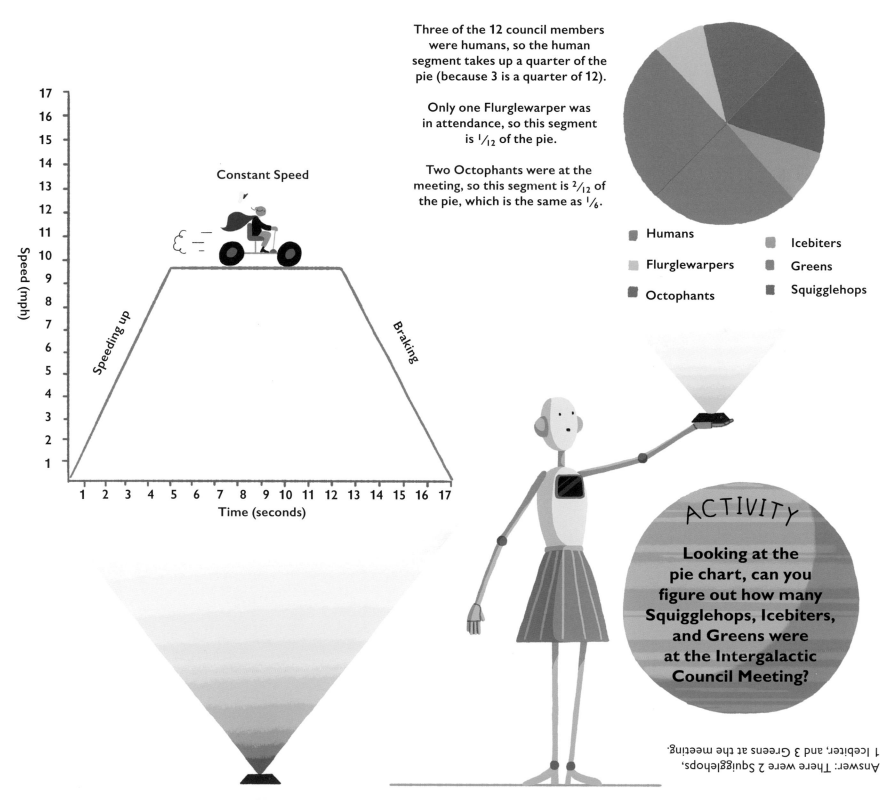

Three of the 12 council members were humans, so the human segment takes up a quarter of the pie (because 3 is a quarter of 12).

Only one Flurglewarper was in attendance, so this segment is $1/12$ of the pie.

Two Octophants were at the meeting, so this segment is $2/12$ of the pie, which is the same as $1/6$.

Constant Speed

Speeding up

Braking

Speed (mph)

Time (seconds)

- Humans
- Flurglewarpers
- Octophants
- Icebiters
- Greens
- Squigglehops

ACTIVITY

Looking at the pie chart, can you figure out how many Squigglehops, Icebiters, and Greens were at the Intergalactic Council Meeting?

Answer: There were 2 Squigglehops, 1 Icebiter, and 3 Greens at the meeting.

Lesson 38
What Is Probability?

Will the sun rise tomorrow? Will I win the lottery? Will Adam ask for seconds at dinnertime? To find the answer, you need to understand probability, which is another way of saying how likely something is.

There is a probability scale, which goes from 0 to 1. If something is impossible, it won't happen, so its probability is 0%, or zero out of one (which we write as $^0/_1$), or plain old 0. If something is certain, this means it will definitely happen, so we say its probability is 100%, $^1/_1$, or simply 1. Everything else can be found somewhere along the scale. If something is very likely to happen, we say it has a high probability. If something is very unlikely to happen, we say it has a low probability.

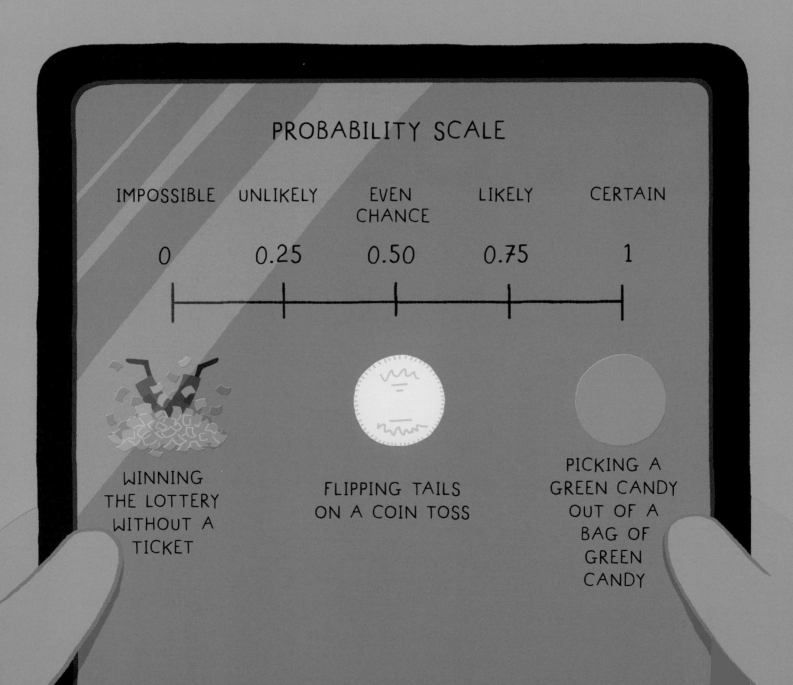

PROBABILITY SCALE

IMPOSSIBLE	UNLIKELY	EVEN CHANCE	LIKELY	CERTAIN
0	0.25	0.50	0.75	1

WINNING THE LOTTERY WITHOUT A TICKET

FLIPPING TAILS ON A COIN TOSS

PICKING A GREEN CANDY OUT OF A BAG OF GREEN CANDY

Take a look at my gizmo gobstopper dispenser. When I pull the lever, a gobstopper gets picked at random. There are 10 gobstoppers in total, and 8 of them are blue, so the probability of picking a blue gobstopper is $^8/_{10}$, 0.8, or 80%, meaning it is quite likely.

Some probability puzzles baffle even top mathematicians! Imagine I have three upside-down cups: A, B, and C. Under one of them is a Saturn gold coin. I ask you to choose a cup—let's imagine you choose cup B. At this point, there's a $^1/_3$ chance that the cup you've chosen is the one with the coin, right? Then I lift up cup C, showing you that it's empty. I'm now going to ask if you'd like to change your mind: will you stick with cup B, or will you switch to cup A?

You may think that it doesn't make a difference—that the probability of the coin being under cup A is the same as the probability of the coin being under cup B: $^1/_3$. But that's where you're wrong! At this point, the probability of the coin being under cup A is $^2/_3$, while the probability of the coin being under cup B is still only $^1/_3$. You should switch cups. It sounds bizarre, but this illustration shows you how the math works.

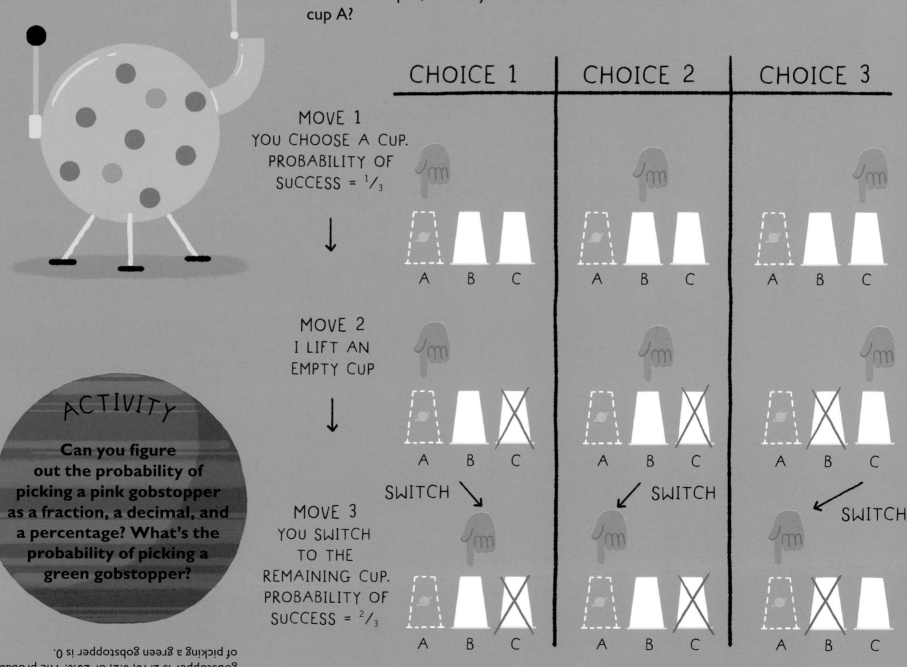

MOVE 1
YOU CHOOSE A CUP.
PROBABILITY OF
SUCCESS = $^1/_3$

MOVE 2
I LIFT AN
EMPTY CUP

SWITCH

MOVE 3
YOU SWITCH
TO THE
REMAINING CUP.
PROBABILITY OF
SUCCESS = $^2/_3$

CHOICE 1 | CHOICE 2 | CHOICE 3

A B C | A B C | A B C

YOU DON'T GET THE COIN. | YOU GET THE COIN! | YOU GET THE COIN!

ACTIVITY

Can you figure out the probability of picking a pink gobstopper as a fraction, a decimal, and a percentage? What's the probability of picking a green gobstopper?

Answer: The probability of picking a pink gobstopper is 2/10, 0.2, or 20%. The probability of picking a green gobstopper is 0.

Lesson 39
Maps and Compasses

Have you ever wondered what a compass would point to in space? The answer is, not much. A compass works using a magnetic field. Planet Earth is like a big magnet, because its core is made up mainly of iron. This magnetic core creates a large magnetic field. If you're within range of Earth's magnetic field, then your compass will point to Earth's magnetic north pole. But if you're out of reach of any planet or star's magnetic field, then your compass isn't going to be any use. But map-reading and compass skills are still essential to your training: you will certainly need them when touching down on new planets.

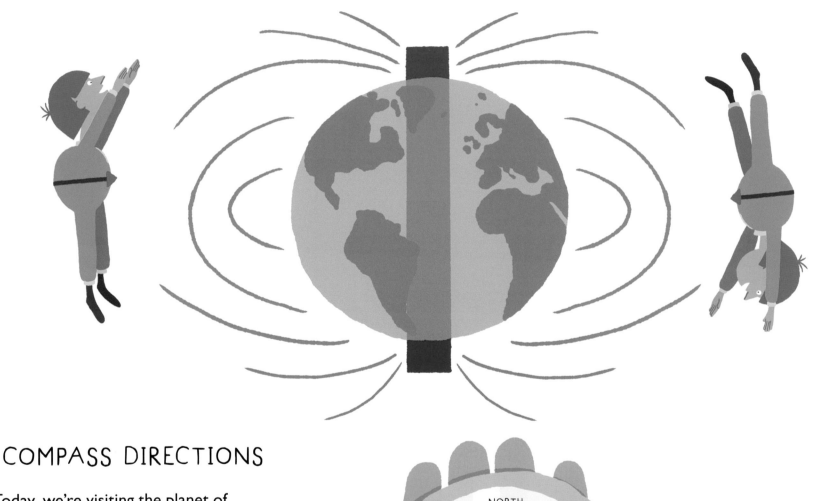

COMPASS DIRECTIONS

Today, we're visiting the planet of Novaterra. You will each be armed with a map and a compass. There are eight main compass points. **The red end of a compass needle always points north**, so if you can align the red needle with the "N" on your compass, you'll be able to figure out which way is which.

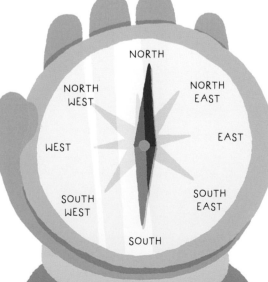

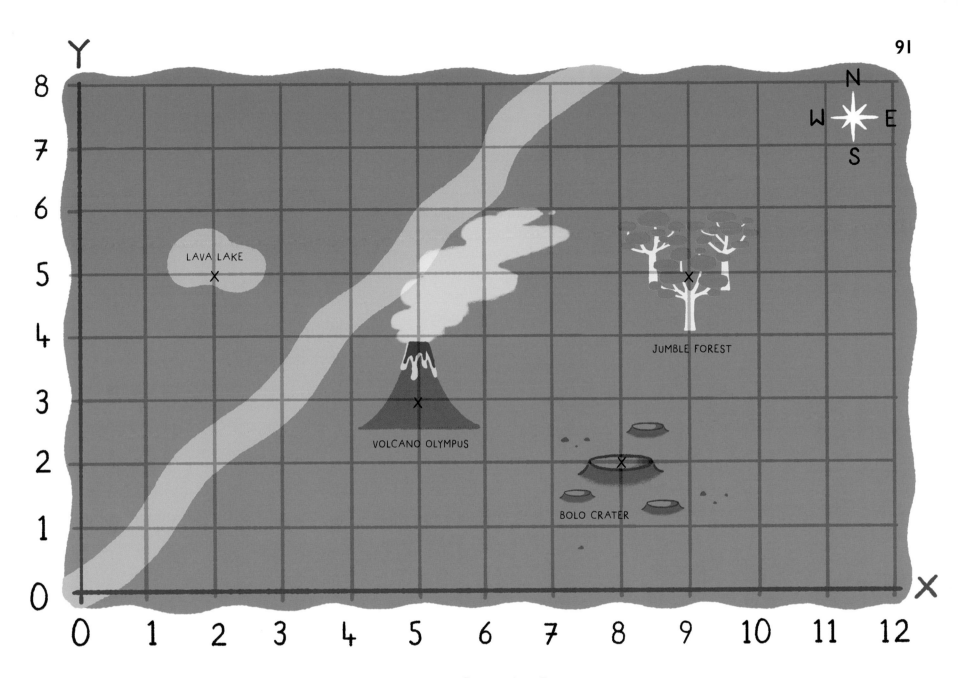

COORDINATES

If we start at the Lava Lake and walk three square east, then two squares south, we end up at Volcano Olympus. If we start at the Jumble Forest and walk three squares south and one square west, we end up at the Bolo Crater.

STRANGE BUT TRUE

Most maps have north at the top, but it hasn't always been this way. Many ancient maps put east at the top, as this is where the sun rises.

Your map has an X axis along the bottom, and a Y axis up the side. We have been given a list of several important locations on the planet's surface, for which we need to note down the map coordinates. What are the coordinates of the Lava Lake? First, we look along the X axis, then we read up the Y axis. The Lava Lake's coordinates are (2, 5).

ACTIVITY

Can you note down the map coordinates for the rest of these Novaterra landmarks?
1. Volcano Olympus
2. Jumble Tree Forest
3. Bolo Crater

Answers: 1. (5, 3), 2. (9, 5), 3. (8, 2)

Lesson 40
Mission to Mars

We've reached our final lesson together, my dear cadets. What a journey it's been! For our last lesson we're going to use our math skills to plot a course from Earth to Mars. What do you think will be the easiest way to travel there? A straight line? Not

in the case of interplanetary travel! When we are close to a star or planet, its gravity exercises a pull on our spacecraft, holding us in orbit around it. We would need masses of fuel to overcome this gravity. The best route will work with gravity to get us to our

destination without using up too much fuel. This is called an **orbital transfer**, and involves shifting from Earth's orbit to the orbit of Mars. It requires a good knowledge of geometry!

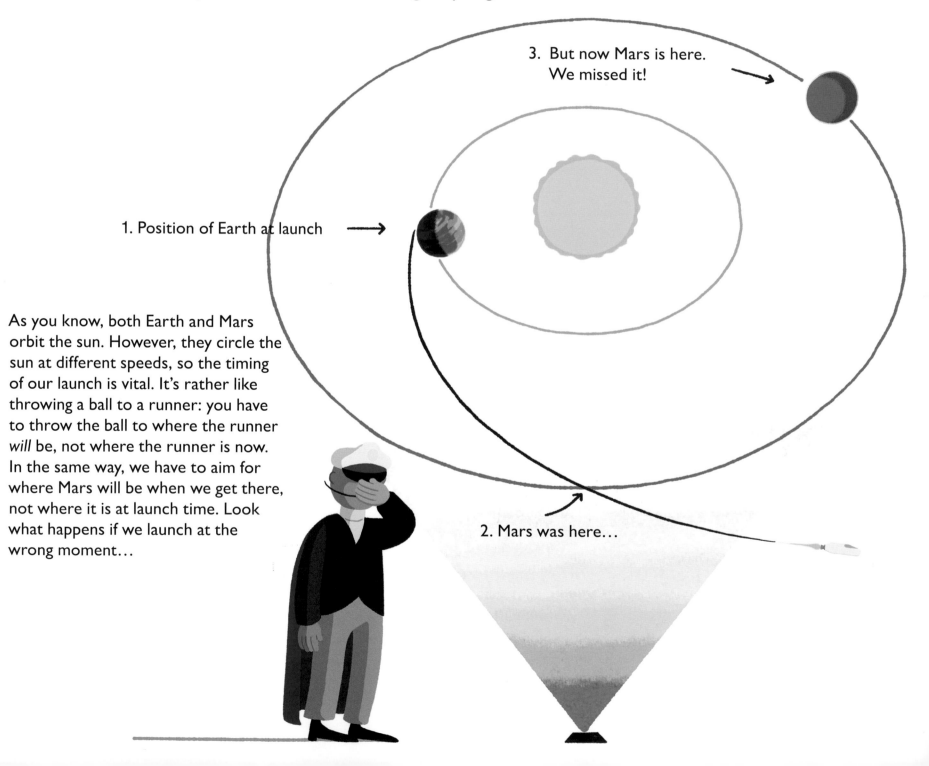

1. Position of Earth at launch →

3. But now Mars is here. We missed it!

2. Mars was here…

As you know, both Earth and Mars orbit the sun. However, they circle the sun at different speeds, so the timing of our launch is vital. It's rather like throwing a ball to a runner: you have to throw the ball to where the runner *will* be, not where the runner is now. In the same way, we have to aim for where Mars will be when we get there, not where it is at launch time. Look what happens if we launch at the wrong moment…

We must plot our course carefully so that our arrival ties in with Mars's orbit. Earth and Mars align for this kind of orbital transfer once every 26 months. We'd better not miss our chance!

If we travel at a speed of roughly 40 million miles per month, and our curved route to Mars is 300 million miles, how many months will it take us to reach our destination?

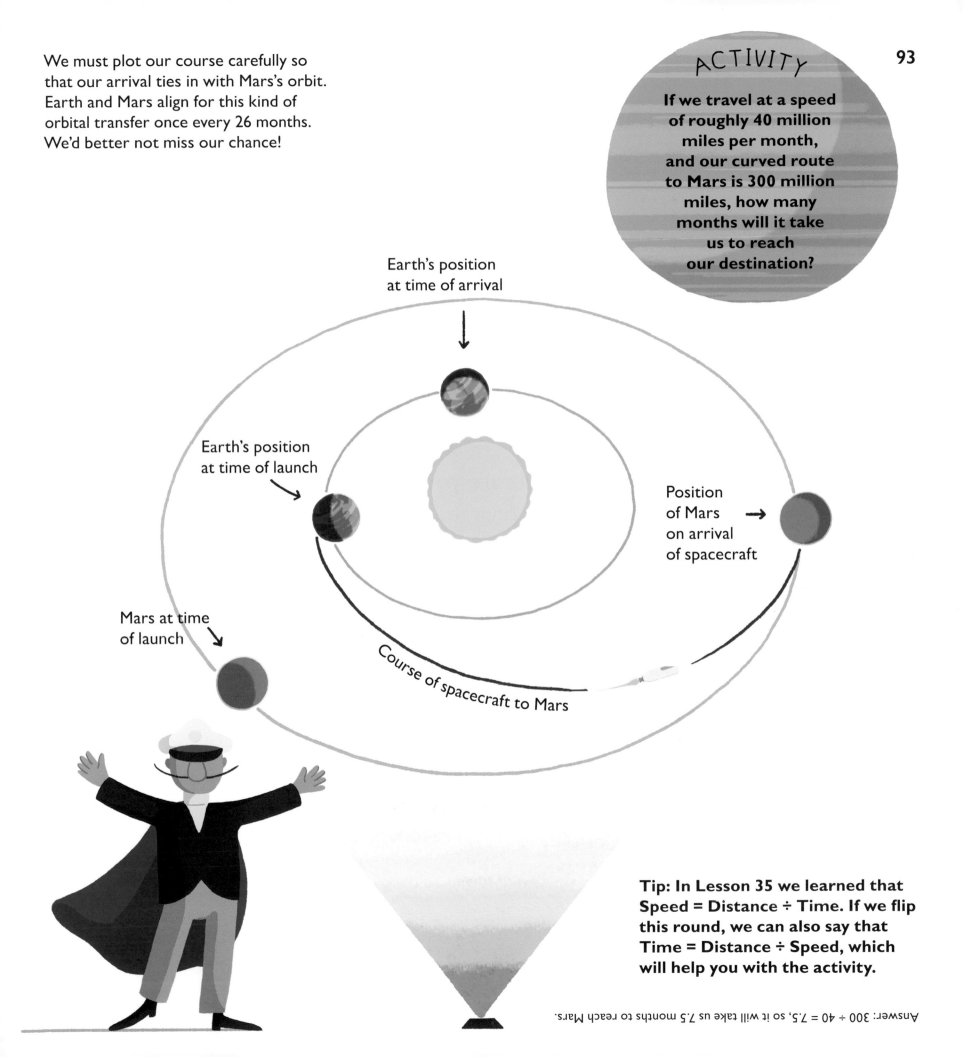

Earth's position at time of arrival

Earth's position at time of launch

Position of Mars on arrival of spacecraft

Mars at time of launch

Course of spacecraft to Mars

Tip: In Lesson 35 we learned that Speed = Distance ÷ Time. If we flip this round, we can also say that Time = Distance ÷ Speed, which will help you with the activity.

Answer: 300 ÷ 40 = 7.5, so it will take us 7.5 months to reach Mars.

Graduation Ceremony

Well done, cadets. You've reached the end of your third and final term at the Astro Academy, which means you're ready to become official crewmembers of the *Starship Infinity*. It's time to celebrate your achievements at our graduation ceremony—congratulations!

Math is a living, breathing subject. It may seem that the experts have all the answers, and that there's not much more to find out. But the more we discover about math, the world, and the cosmos, the more we realize how much there still is to learn. Mathematicians today are grappling with many big questions, such as what is the next largest prime number, how big is infinity, and what is the shape of the universe?

Your voyage of mathematical discovery is by no means over—it's only just beginning!

Brimming with creative inspiration, how-to projects, and useful information to enrich your everyday life, Quarto Knows is a favorite destination for those pursuing their interests and passions. Visit our site and dig deeper with our books into your area of interest: Quarto Creates, Quarto Cooks, Quarto Homes, Quarto Lives, Quarto Drives, Quarto Explores, Quarto Gifts, or Quarto Kids.

The publishers and authors would like to thank Melissa Gibson for her invaluable advice and support as consultant for this book.

The School of Numbers © 2019 Quarto Publishing plc. Text © 2019 Emily Hawkins. Illustrations © 2019 Daniel Frost.

First Published in 2019 by Wide Eyed Editions, an imprint of The Quarto Group.
400 First Avenue North, Suite 400, Minneapolis MN 55401, USA
www.QuartoKnows.com

The right of Daniel Frost to be identified as the illustrator and Emily Hawkins to be identified as the author of this work has been asserted by them in accordance with the Copyright, Designs and Patents Act, 1988 (United Kingdom).

A catalog record for this book is available from the British Library.

ISBN 978-1-78603-184-6

The illustrations were created digitally
Set in Gill Sans

Published by Rachel Williams and Jenny Broom
Designed by Joe Hales
Edited by Jenny Broom and Claire Grace
Production by Kate O'Riordan and Jenny Cundill

Manufactured in Shenzhen, China PP112020

9 8 7 6 5 4

BOOKS THAT HAVE INSPIRED US

ALEX'S ADVENTURES IN NUMBERLAND, ALEX BELLOS (BLOOMSBURY, 2010)
For older readers and adults, this fascinating book reveals how math underpins just about everything we do.

THE BIG QUESTIONS: MATHEMATICS, TONY CRILLY (QUERCUS, 2011)
Another book for older readers and adults, this thought-provoking guide confronts the thorny questions that have puzzled mathematicians for generations.

MARVELLOUS MATHS, JONATHAN LITTON AND THOMAS FLINTHAM (TEMPLAR PUBLISHING, 2013)
An interactive exploration of math, with pop-ups, flaps, and pull-tabs.

THE SECRET OF SUMS, KJARTAN POSKITT (SCHOLASTIC, 2014)
A wonderful, witty, whistle-stop tour through the world of numbers.

ALL SHAPES AND SIZES, KJARTAN POSKITT (SCHOLASTIC, 2014)
A super-fun exploration of all things shape-related.

777 MATHEMATICAL CONVERSATION STARTERS, JOHN DE PILLIS (THE MATHEMATICAL ASSOCIATION OF AMERICA, 2004)
Many thanks to Professor de Pillis for his kind permission to reproduce his brilliant probability diagram on page 89.